never alone

WALKING WITH GOD
THROUGH DEPRESSION

AUBREY COLEMAN & JOY WOO

Study Suggestions

We believe that the Bible is true, trustworthy, and timeless and that it is vitally important for all believers. These study suggestions are intended to help you more effectively study Scripture as you seek to know and love God through His Word.

SUGGESTED STUDY TOOLS

- A Bible

- A double-spaced, printed copy of the Scripture passages that this study covers. You can use a website like *www.biblegateway.com* to copy the text of a passage and print out a double-spaced copy to be able to mark on easily.

- A journal to write notes or prayers

- Pens, colored pencils, and highlighters

- A dictionary to look up unfamiliar words

HOW TO USE THIS STUDY

Begin your study time in prayer. Ask God to reveal Himself to you, to help you understand what you are reading, and to transform you with His Word (Psalm 119:18).

Before you read what is written in each day of the study itself, read the assigned passages of Scripture for that day. Use your double-spaced copy to circle, underline, highlight, draw arrows, and mark in any way you would like to help you dig deeper as you work through a passage.

Read the daily written content provided for the current study day.

Answer the questions that appear at the end of each study day.

The inductive method provides tools for deeper and more intentional Bible study. To study a book of the Bible inductively, work through the steps below after reading background information on the book.

1 OBSERVATION & COMPREHENSION
Key question: What does the text say?

After reading the book of the Bible in its entirety at least once, begin working with smaller portions of the book. Read a passage of Scripture repetitively, and then mark the following items in the text:

- Key or repeated words and ideas
- Key themes
- Transition words (*Ex: therefore, but, because, if/then, likewise, etc.*)
- Lists
- Comparisons & Contrasts
- Commands
- Unfamiliar words (look these up in a dictionary)
- Questions you have about the text

2 INTERPRETATION
Key question: What does the text mean?

Once you have annotated the text, work through the following steps to help you interpret its meaning:

- Read the passage in other versions for a better understanding of the text.
- Read cross-references to help interpret Scripture with Scripture.
- Paraphrase or summarize the passage to check for understanding.
- Identify how the text reflects the metanarrative of Scripture, which is the story of creation, fall, redemption, and restoration.
- Read trustworthy commentaries if you need further insight into the meaning of the passage.

3

APPLICATION
Key Question: How should the truth of this passage change me?

Bible study is not merely an intellectual pursuit. The truths about God, ourselves, and the gospel that we discover in Scripture should produce transformation in our hearts and lives. Answer the following questions as you consider what you have learned in your study:

- What attributes of God's character are revealed in the passage?

  Consider places where the text directly states the character of God, as well as how His character is revealed through His words and actions.

- What do I learn about myself in light of who God is?

  Consider how you fall short of God's character, how the text reveals your sin nature, and what it says about your new identity in Christ.

- How should this truth change me?

  A passage of Scripture may contain direct commands telling us what to do or warnings about sins to avoid in order to help us grow in holiness. Other times our application flows out of seeing ourselves in light of God's character. As we pray and reflect on how God is calling us to change in light of His Word, we should be asking questions like, "How should I pray for God to change my heart?" and "What practical steps can I take toward cultivating habits of holiness?"

ATTRIBUTES OF GOD

ETERNAL

God has no beginning and no end. He always was, always is, and always will be.

HAB 1:12 / REV. 1:8 / IS. 41:4

FAITHFUL

God is incapable of anything but fidelity. He is loyally devoted to His plan and purpose.

2 TIM. 2:13 / DEUT. 7:9
HEB. 10:23

GLORIOUS

God is ultimately beautiful, deserving of all praise and honor.

REV. 19:1 / PS. 104:1
EX. 40:34-35

GOOD

God is pure; there is no defilement in Him. He is unable to sin, and all He does is good.

GEN. 1:31 / PS. 34:8 / PS. 107:1

GRACIOUS

God is kind, giving to us gifts and benefits which we are undeserving of.

2 KINGS 13:23 / PS. 145:8
IS. 30:18

HOLY

God is undefiled and unable to be in the presence of defilement. He is sacred and set-apart.

REV. 4:8 / LEV. 19:2 / HAB. 1:13

IMMUTABLE

God does not change. He is the same yesterday, today, and tomorrow.

1 SAM. 15:29 / ROM. 11:29
JAMES 1:17

JEALOUS

God is desirous of receiving the praise and affection He rightly deserves.

EX. 20:5 / DEUT. 4:23-24
JOSH. 24:19

JUST

God governs in perfect justice. He acts in accordance with justice. In Him there is no wrongdoing or dishonesty.

IS. 61:8 / DEUT. 32:4 / PS. 146:7-9

LOVE

God is eternally, enduringly, steadfastly loving and affectionate. He does not forsake or betray His covenant love.

JN. 3:16 / EPH. 2:4-5 / 1 JN. 4:16

MERCIFUL

God is compassionate, withholding us from the wrath that we are deserving of.

TITUS 3:5 / PS. 25:10
LAM. 3:22-23

OMNIPOTENT

God is all-powerful; His strength is unlimited.

MAT. 19:26 / JOB 42:1-2
JER. 32:27

OMNIPRESENT

God is everywhere; His presence is near and permeating.

PROV. 15:3 / PS. 139:7-10
JER. 23:23-24

OMNISCIENT

God is all-knowing; there is nothing unknown to Him.

PS. 147:4 / I JN. 3:20
HEB. 4:13

PATIENT

God is long-suffering and enduring. He gives ample opportunity for people to turn toward Him.

ROM. 2:4 / 2 PET. 3:9 / PS. 86:15

RIGHTEOUS

God is blameless and upright. There is no wrong found in Him.

PS. 119:137 / JER. 12:1
REV. 15:3

SOVEREIGN

God governs over all things; He is in complete control.

COL. 1:17 / PS. 24:1-2
1 CHRON. 29:11-12

TRUE

God is our measurement of what is fact. By Him are we able to discern true and false.

JN. 3:33 / ROM. 1:25 / JN. 14:6

WISE

God is infinitely knowledgeable and is judicious with His knowledge.

IS. 46:9-10 / IS. 55:9 / PROV. 3:19

METANARRATIVE OF SCRIPTURE

Creation

In the beginning, God created the universe. He made the world and everything in it. He created humans in His own image to be His representatives on the earth.

Fall

The first humans, Adam and Eve, disobeyed God by eating from the fruit of the Tree of Knowledge of Good and Evil. Because of sin, the world was cursed. The punishment for sin is death, and because of Adam's original sin, all humans are sinful and condemned to death.

Redemption

God sent his Son to become a human and redeem His people. Jesus Christ lived a sinless life but died on the cross to pay the penalty for sin. He resurrected from the dead and ascended into heaven. All who put their faith in Jesus are saved from death and freely receive the gift of eternal life.

Restoration

One day, Jesus Christ will return again and restore all that sin destroyed. He will usher in a new heaven and new earth where all who trust in Him will live eternally with glorified bodies in the presence of God.

table of contents

extras

DISCLAIMER

-

Any diagnosis of clinical depression must come from a medical professional who is qualified to diagnose and treat such physiological symptoms. You should never attempt to self-diagnose. If you think you may be struggling with clinical depression, please seek the help of a qualified mental health professional. We hope that this study will be an encouragement to you regardless of the nature of your depression, as God and His word speak to every condition, physical or spiritual. And we can cling to His Word even as we partake of the physical blessings of professional help and means of care that He provides to meet specific needs that we have.

NO CIRCUMSTANCE, OR LACK THEREOF,
CAN SHAKE THE POWER OF YOUR
SAVIOR AND HIS LOVE FOR YOU,
EVEN WHEN YOU DO NOT FEEL IT.

week 1 | day 1

introduction

Read: Psalm 102

Depression. For some, it feels like such a heavy weight to carry that they are unable to step out of bed in the morning. For others, it feels like a prison sentence, a trap, or a bad nightmare from which they are unable to wake up. For others still, it feels like nothing—numbness is their coping mechanism and constant reality. It manifests itself in ways as unique as the individuals it haunts. From the wealthiest, seemingly happiest people on earth, to the poorest and lowest of every culture, anyone can experience depression, even Christians. Depression can be a confusing, burdensome pit or a journey orienting our gaze increasingly to our Savior.

Depression is characterized by constant or prolonged feelings of worthlessness, guilt, emptiness, or hopelessness that interferes with one's ability to carry out normal, daily activities. It can also result in a diminished motivation to perform simple life tasks like getting out of bed, eating, working, caring for family members, or spending time with friends. This is what we mean when we refer to depression throughout this study. God has designed humans as psychosomatic creatures, which means that we are mind, body, and soul all at the same time. None of these elements can be separated from one another, and they each feed into and affect one another. This means that there can be physical or biological influences contributing to depression too. For this reason, there is what is called clinical depression caused by chemical imbalances in the body which can be aided by medication. However, not all depression is clinical.

Depression can also be circumstantial or other times occur seemingly without cause. Some struggle with specific grief and thoughts related to identifiable and often recent events that have led them to wrestle with what is known as circumstantial depression. Circumstantial depression can be related to trauma or loss, sin or perceived guilt, and a variety of other circumstances. In this case, someone struggling with depression can typically verbalize the cause or reason for his or her pain. Causeless depression, on the other hand, typically means that the person cannot verbalize a specific cause or reason for sadness, but it does not mean that there is not one. As we will learn, all depression has a single source. Whether the roots are primarily biological or not, all depression has spiritual factors and is something that the Lord can enter into with us.

Because it tends to lead to feelings of hopelessness and perpetual sadness, Christians often accuse other Christians of sinning by their experience with depression, but this is a dangerous myth. The truth is that even Jesus who was without sin struggled with feelings of depression, as did many faithful men and women throughout Scripture. We will trace their stories together in this study. This broken world is aching and, rightly, so do we. Depression is not something to be ashamed of or to feel guilt over. If you are dealing with thoughts and feelings of depression, know that it is not a sin and that you are never alone in the journey.

The purpose of this study is to come alongside those of you fighting the battle of depression, whether personally or alongside a friend, spouse, or another family member who is struggling in this fight. This resource is neither a diagnosis nor a prognosis but is meant to be a companion along the road for those who are fighting daily to see the light through the darkness haunting their minds. The goal is that you might see Jesus extending tender, loving arms toward you in your sorrow, numbness, or fear. Our study will be descriptive rather than prescriptive as we see various ways that depression can manifest, play out, and come to an end. Every journey is unique, and the Lord heals in His time and in His way. As we learn to cling to God's promises more and more, day by day, the goal is not that all the problems in our lives melt away, or even that the depression ceases, but that we might find Christ a comfort amid the path through all these things.

For many who are depressed, nothing seems to matter anymore; even if they know there is a purpose, that purpose can be hard to feel. If that is you, all the above words of hope and encouragement may have sounded familiar and simply fallen flat to your ears. Maybe you have wrestled with depression for many years, and your faith is beginning to feel shaky, or maybe the depression has only just begun, and it makes you wonder if all you believed before was true. Hear this, friend: no circumstance, or lack thereof, can shake the power of your Savior and His love for you, even when you do not feel it. The name of your depression may be defined by your circumstances, but your God is not. May you see that He and His Word define you and your life, not this darkness that weighs on your soul.

As Hebrews 4:15 reminds us, Jesus experienced all the pain and brokenness of this world when He came to earth as a man. He entered into our heartache, taking it on Himself. His heart and body were broken for us, not only when He bore our sin on the cross but as He walked and lived among us. Scripture tells us that Jesus' own soul was troubled at times too (John 12:27). If you have trusted Christ as your Savior, there is no sorrow or grief you have known that Jesus does not understand and mourn with you. If you are fighting guilt over sin, He grieves your sin with you. He died to join you in that fight. If you are struggling with feelings of worthlessness or hopelessness, remember that Jesus loved you before there was anything lovely in you. He was scorned and rejected by all to give meaning and value to your life. If you are feeling overwhelmingly sad without any clear reason, Jesus is near to you in your brokenheartedness (Psalm 34:18). He came to begin the end of all brokenness and invites you to Himself that you might know full and final healing in Him someday in heaven and every day after. He is the best companion and light through this present darkness.

What brings you to this study? Whether for personal use or to aid your ministry to a friend, what do you hope to learn through this study?

_____

_____

_____

_____

_____

_____

_____

How do the mentioned characterizations of depression resonate with you?

_____

_____

_____

_____

_____

_____

_____

Pray and ask God to comfort and strengthen you through His Word as you walk through this study.

_____

_____

_____

_____

_____

_____

THE BIBLE SPEAKS OF A
BEGINNING WE ALL ACHE
FOR — NO SIN, NO SHAME,
NO FEAR, AND NO SORROW.

why do we have depression?

Read: Genesis 1:28-31, Genesis 3:17-19, Romans 5:18, Romans 8:18-23

When God created the world, He did so perfectly. He created everything with purpose and intention—His thoughtful hand woven into the waves of the sea, the stars in the sky, the fruitful land, animals of every species, and the heart of mankind. Made in the image of God, Adam and Eve were placed in the flourishing and fruitful garden of Eden to enjoy it and to live. Reflecting God like no other creation, man was in a state of emotional bliss, for all that God had created was very good, and man lived in sinless innocence with Him. Adam and Eve were content and cared for in every way, and they were provided with everything they needed because they lived in the presence of God.

The Bible speaks of a beginning we all ache for—no sin, no shame, no fear, and no sorrow. But Adam and Eve rejected the truth about God in exchange for a deadly lie that would result in the fall of man and separate them from the presence of God. Their emotional, physical, and spiritual bliss turned to agony. They were afraid, ashamed, and guilt-ridden. They turned on one another and sought to hide from God. Their lives were turned upside down, and all that God deemed good was distorted by their sin. Life outside of Eden brought pain and difficulty for every generation that followed. The result of the fall was costly and had catastrophic effects on the way we function and live in this world.

Those who suffer from depression can find their why in ramifications of the fall, with consequences affecting their entire being. Depression is multifaceted and complicated. It is a result of the fallen nature of man. Our bodies of death, as Paul refers to them in Romans 7:24, bear the effects of sin all on their own. Chemical and hormonal imbalances, injury or illness, heartache or stress, and battles of the flesh all contribute to the physical display of depression. Additionally, our minds, emotions, and ways of perceiving our realities are distorted by sin. Ephesians 2:3 reminds us that as a result of the fall, we all live according to the desires of our flesh, carrying out the distorted and deceitful motives of the body and mind. Familiar to those who face depression head-on, it is fueled by perpetual and unrelenting negative thoughts, feelings, and beliefs about God and ourselves. We can easily become consumed in our own darkness or send ourselves into a spiral of doubt if we have nothing else to tell us otherwise.

The looming effects of the fall would leave us hopeless if that were the end of the story. But thanks be to God, it is not. The groaning pains of this world point us beyond what is earthly. From the very beginning, God held a redemptive plan for His people to reverse the curse of sin. He would send a Savior who would take all that was broken and distorted by sin and make it new. Someone had to pay the price for all that was lost in the fall, but that someone required a righteousness that no mere man could achieve. Therefore, God sent His perfect Son, Jesus Christ, to step into the sorrow and sin of this world, to live righteously, to bear the wrath of God on the cross, and to defeat sin once and for all. He suffered so we might be set free from suffering. He came low to the point of death to raise us up in new life with Him. This is the glorious news of the gospel.

Through salvation in Christ, we are sealed with the promise of a day when all things wrong will be made right—a day when we will be united with Christ in the heavenly realms and invited into the presence of God. Our minds and bodies will be restored. We will no longer be riddled with imbalances, imperfections, or internal failings. We will no longer be misguided and deceived by our hearts and minds. We will no longer bear the weight of sorrow, trauma, anguish, or sin. Depression and every discouraging and devastating reverberation of the fall will be no more.

As we wait for that glorious day, we continue to live in the consequences of the fall. But we wait with hope. We are reminded in Scripture that Christ's strength is revealed in our weaknesses. Limping toward heaven, we have an opportunity to embrace the gospel-saving working of Jesus Christ in our hearts, minds, and souls in a transformative way. The same power that brings life from death is accessible and at work in all who find their hope and salvation in Jesus Christ. Our grief and sorrows can serve as a means of bringing us closer to Him. Though we suffer, we know He has purchased peace and joy for us on the horizon. We are sustained by that which is unseen yet eternal. Psalm 73:26 affirms, "My flesh and my heart may fail, but God is the strength of my heart, my portion forever." Nothing can separate us from what is promised in Christ, including the physical, emotional, and spiritual suffering that accompanies depression.

We wait with expectation for the culmination of Christ's promise where we find untamable joy, unsearchable comfort, and the unending presence of God. The truth for Christians is not that we will be exempt from such things as depression, but it does mean we can walk through it differently with Christ. There is an end for all who battle days, seasons, or even a lifetime of depression, but that end is only found in the eternal hope of Jesus Christ. May we run to Him today with full assurance that He will greet us graciously and expectantly with open arms.

"HE SUFFERED SO WE MIGHT BE SET FREE FROM SUFFERING."

Read Genesis 1:28-31 and Genesis 3:17-19. Compare the two passages. What effect did Adam and Eve's disobedience have?

_____

_____

_____

_____

_____

_____

Read Romans 8:18-23. List every description of creation in this passage. How do these descriptions explain why we might battle with depression?

_____

_____

_____

_____

_____

_____

What hope do we have for the redemption of creation? What comfort does this bring?

_____

_____

_____

_____

_____

_____

OUR GREATEST HOPE
FOR WALKING THROUGH
DEPRESSION IS WALKING
WITH GOD.

elijah's story

Read: 1 Kings 18

The pages of the Bible reveal that many men and women experienced depression during their lifetime. There we find stories riddled with scars and sorrows, tears and trepidation, defeat and discouragement, even among the most faithful. Among them, we find a well-known case for depression in the life of the prophet Elijah who we remember as a courageous man of the Old Testament. A deeper look into his life and circumstances reveals that it was not one thing but many that contributed to Elijah wrestling through depression.

In 1 Kings 18, Elijah was living and serving during the days of King Ahab and his queen, Jezebel, who wickedly introduced Baal worship to Israel. As a response, Elijah was chosen by God as a vessel for change, to challenge the king and the prophets of Baal, and to call the nation back from apostasy. This was a mighty charge, a significant burden and weight that Elijah would hold, but he accepted it willingly. Elijah went to the king and invited all of Israel and the false prophets to join him on Mt. Carmel. Through this encounter on the mountain, Elijah confronted them for being spiritually lukewarm. They could not decide whether to worship God or to worship Baal. So, Elijah challenged the 450 prophets of Baal by saying, "Then you call on the name of your god, and I will call on the name of the Lord. The God who answers with fire, he is God" (1 Kings 18:24). Baal's prophets accepted the challenge, set up their altar, and began crying to their god. But no fire fell. Elijah suggested they shout louder. And when still no fire fell, Elijah mocked, "Maybe he's thinking it over; maybe he has wandered away; or maybe he's on the road. Perhaps he's sleeping and will wake up!" (1 Kings 18:27). As a final appeal, Baal's prophets slashed themselves with knives, but that did not work either. No fire came. After all this, Elijah built an altar to the Lord, dug a trench around it, and ordered water to be poured over it. Then Elijah prayed a simple prayer, and God sent fire to consume the sacrifice, altar, and water. The people worshiped the Lord and shouted, "The Lord, he is God! The Lord, he is God!" (1 Kings 18:39). And everyone knew God's hand was upon Elijah. Through this monumental encounter, Elijah was God's instrument in challenging and successfully proving to Israel that the Lord is the only true God worthy of their worship.

We might assume after such a victory that Elijah would have been elated, full of joy, and celebrating. Elijah was not permitted to relish the mountain-top experience long, however. As soon as Queen Jezebel heard what happened, she sent Elijah a message saying that by the next day, she was going to kill him. When the prophet of God read her message, his heart sank, and he began to run for his life. He ran to Beersheba, the southernmost city in Judah, which was essentially the end of civilization. It was surrounded by desert, so on the next day's journey, he found himself in the wilderness alone. As he ran away from all that he had known, Elijah found himself under a juniper tree asking God to take his life.

We may be surprised by these circumstances, or we might find them completely relatable to our own. Coming from the highest of highs to the lowest of lows, how could Elijah find himself in such a state of depression? We are tempted to look upon men like Elijah as untouchable saints—those unfettered by the hard and difficult. But in reality, he was human, made up of the same weaknesses, frailties, and emotions found in all of us. It is important to remember that depression touches even those it seems it could never reach. Depression does not always come with a warning sign or time to prepare. Sometimes it catches us off guard in the most unexpected moments of life and in ways we may have never imagined. Elijah's story will help us strip away our faulty assumptions regarding depression, equipping us with God's Word to better understand it for ourselves and to better serve and comfort others who are battling depression.

Over the next couple of days in this study, we will look more closely at the symptoms and influences of Elijah's depression. Elijah's depression was not bound to any one cause, and it is important to look into each element of his experience to help us better understand and articulate our own. As we continue looking to the pages of the Bible for a greater understanding of depression and how we see it in the lives of God's people, we must also closely draw our attention to seeing God amid the sin and suffering of His people. Our greatest hope for walking through depression is walking with God. Though Elijah felt alone and abandoned, God remained near and present. With steady assurance, Elijah first began proclaiming the message to Ahab that God entrusted to him, saying, "As the Lord of Armies lives, in whose presence I stand…" (1 Kings 18:15), and we see God's grand display of this reality on Mt. Carmel. But even in the aftermath, we are reminded that "the power of the Lord was on Elijah"(1 Kings 18:46). Throughout the story of Elijah and the ones that follow, we will notice that no matter the reasoning, God remains in their midst. The promise of Immanuel, which means "God is with us," is fulfilled in Jesus Christ who made a way to dwell among us. He stopped at nothing to bring His presence near. May our hearts be secure knowing that even when walking through valleys of depression and despair, the people of God will never walk alone.

How do you resonate with the introduction to Elijah?

_____

_____

_____

_____

_____

_____

_____

How might Elijah's story change assumptions that surround depression?

_____

_____

_____

_____

_____

_____

_____

In what ways do you see God presently at work in Elijah's circumstances?
In what ways do you see God presently at work in the midst of yours?

_____

_____

_____

_____

_____

_____

EVEN WHEN OUR THOUGHTS
AND HEARTS CONDEMN US, GOD
IS GREATER THAN OUR HEARTS.

elijah: fear and low view of self

Read: 1 Kings 19:1-4

Elijah, frightened by the death threats of Jezebel, ran for his life immediately following the victorious display on Mt. Carmel. This is the beginning of what we can identify as Elijah's battle with depression. One of the ways depression can be enhanced or provoked is by fear. In Elijah's case, there was a viable reason for Him to be afraid. His life was at stake. He felt that there was no way to avoid the death threats presented by Jezebel who had such power and authority over him. Everything about his life that was known and normal up to that point had changed. He likely felt as if he had nowhere to go and no one to help him escape Jezebel's vengeance. By running away, Elijah isolated himself from those who were closest to him and everything that once made him feel grounded and secure. He turned inward for strength and comfort, even after God had displayed His presence to Him in such a powerful way. His fear was blinding him in such a way that He felt isolated from the One closest to him.

Fear leads us to pull away from someone or something. It motivates us to avoid whatever it is that makes us feel unsafe or uncertain. There is certainly a healthy kind of fear that encourages caution and evaluation of the given circumstances and scenarios. However, when we become ruled or blinded by fear, it can lead to isolation, avoidance, and excessive doubt. As a result, fear is often accompanied by anxious thoughts. Fear can lead us to run away to escape or to set ourselves free from the thoughts and doubts consuming our minds. Fear and anxiety are driving factors of depression. They bring us to look inwardly to ourselves for security and comfort, which ironically becomes an endless cycle where we find that our best efforts still cannot diminish our fear.

When Elijah finally quit running, exhausted by his efforts, he sat down under a juniper tree and asked God to let him die, saying, "I have had enough! Lord, take my life, for I'm no better than my fathers" (1 Kings 19:4). They had been unsuccessful in stamping out apostasy in Israel, and he felt like a failure of his own. This highlights another element of Elijah's depression—a negative view of himself. He felt he was no more successful in correcting the nation's apostasy than the prophets who had gone before him. He felt discouraged, downcast, and defeated. These views led him to question whether it was even worth running or trying to survive the lingering threats for his life. A low view of self can heighten or encourage depression, feeding the lie that our lives hold no value and that our sheer existence brings about too much trouble and disappointment. We may feel unnoticed or unwanted which is accelerated when we have isolated ourselves from God and others who can point us elsewhere. We may feel weary or worthless which is provoked when we are consumed by our weaknesses and failings.

God's grace abounds, even in our fear and failings. For Elijah, his thoughts and efforts had brought him to a place of desperation, crying out to the Lord. The safest place we can find ourselves in the midst of battling depression is with eyes and hearts turned upward, regardless of our present state of mind. Our hope lies nowhere else. Even when our thoughts and hearts condemn us, God is greater than our hearts. Even when we were most unlovable, God moved heaven and earth to bring us back into the right relationship with Him. We are reminded through the gospel pursuit and the sacrificial death of Christ that we were sought out and desired in love. In doing so, we take on the beauty and righteousness of Christ, with reason to no longer hang our heads in shame. To fight the lies that scream at us from every side that our life holds no purpose, we need truth that pierces through our perceptions and judgments, truth that rebukes, truth that heals. The truth we search for pours out like soothing balm from the Scriptures, and God is always ready and willing to comfort and receive our cries for help. Even when we feel we have found ourselves in the darkest places, just as Elijah found himself, God is nearer than ever. Psalm 34:18 tells us, "The Lord is near the brokenhearted; he saves those crushed in spirit." His nearness is not dependent on us but sheerly on His promise, love, and commitment to His people.

What two elements of depression are revealed through this passage? What lies do they lead us to believe?

_____

_____

_____

_____

_____

How does God's Word speak to our inclination toward fear and anxiety? Reference Isaiah 41:10, Philippians 4:6-7, 1 Peter 5:6-7, John 14:27, and any additional verses that come to mind.

_____

_____

_____

_____

_____

_____

How does God's Word speak to our inclination toward a low view of self? Reference Jeremiah 17:7, Psalm 139:13-14, 2 Corinthians 3:18, 1 Peter 2:9, and any additional verses that come to mind.

_____

_____

_____

_____

_____

THESE BODILY GROANINGS ARE INTENDED
TO DIRECT OUR HEARTS TO THE ONE WHO
SUSTAINS HIMSELF AND WHO PROMISES
TO SUSTAIN US BEYOND EVEN OUR BASIC,
PHYSICAL NEEDS.

week 1 | *day 5*

elijah: fatigue and futility

Read: 1 Kings 19:5-18

Out of sheer, physical exhaustion, Elijah fell asleep. He was emotionally drained and physically exhausted by the day's proceedings. His mind and body needed rest, so he slept. After some time, the Lord sent an angel to wake up Elijah and give him food to eat and water to drink so that his body might be strengthened and refueled. Then he slept again. Once more, the angel woke him and fed him in preparation for a journey to Mt. Horeb where he was instructed by God to journey to get away from the people and pressures that were troubling him. Strengthened by the food, after forty days and forty nights, Elijah finally reached his destination where he entered a cave and spent the night.

Fatigue, especially that which is prolonged, is one of the most common signs of someone who is battling depression. Physical and mental exhaustion can stem from a lack of motivation to eat, drink, energize, or engage in any sort of enjoyable activity. In some regard, thoughts and feelings of depression can leave us in a sort of physical and mental bondage. We may feel trapped and confined by our darkened thoughts, unmotivated to try and move out of them or escape their detriment. The less we refuel and strengthen our bodies, the weaker and more feeble they will inevitably become. When Elijah fled, consumed with fear and hopelessness, he likely thought little of eating or hydrating — to the point that he was fatigued in every way and his body could not go any longer without rest. God's response was simple and necessary and indicates an immediate need that could be met. He sent food for Elijah and encouraged him to sleep. Whether facing depression on our own or walking through it with a friend, sometimes the simplest next step is to eat and sleep. A multitude of decisions can easily overwhelm, but choosing to refuel and rest with food and sleep can help strengthen and serve us for the days ahead. It requires us only to do the very next thing instead of straining our eyes ahead in a way that exacerbates our circumstances.

Mt. Horeb was as far away from Queen Jezebel as Elijah could go after gaining sufficient energy and strength. In the cave where he ended up, he was consumed by self-pity and dark solitude, recounting his fate of doom when God came to him asking, "What are you doing here, Elijah?" God could have easily approached Elijah with instruction and exhortation, but instead, He encourages him to be introspective. The question He poses gets to the heart of the matter, essentially asking Elijah to consider what led him to this place of despair. Elijah responds, "I have been very zealous for the Lord God of Armies, but the Israelites have abandoned your covenant, torn down your altars, and killed your prophets with the sword. I alone am left, and they are looking for me to take my life," (1 Kings 19:10). These words reveal the deeper thoughts behind his despair and discouragement. He felt alone and helpless and held negative expectations for the future. He felt the futility of all of his accomplishments and pursuits, wondering if all had been in vain or if he had seemingly destroyed his life.

Not only did Elijah need physical rest and nourishment, but he also needed spiritual rest in God's sovereignty and spiritual nourishment in what God says to be true about His delight for him. Ironically, when we look at moments when God provides food for His people in the Bible, it is always followed by pointing them to their ultimate need for rest and nourishment in Him. We need God's help both physically and spiritually as we walk through depression. Our minds and bodies are limited. Think of the many ways our bodies signal to us what we need. When we are hungry, it is because we need food and nourishment. When we get tired and sleepy, we need rest and sleep. These bodily responses are a kindness from the Lord to humble us and remind us that we cannot do it all on our own. We cannot physically sustain ourselves no matter how hard we try. Instead, these bodily groanings are intended to direct our hearts to the One who sustains Himself and who promises to sustain us beyond even our basic, physical needs.

This is an essential truth for anyone walking through bouts of trial and hardship—we need God more than anything else. Psalm 46:1 reminds us, "God is our refuge and strength, a helper who is always found in times of trouble." The truth of who God is and what He does for His people brings us restorative strength in our weakness. It turns our eyes away from ourselves and our self-destructive thoughts to a God who sees us, knows us, and delights in helping us.

What two elements of depression are revealed through this passage? What lies do they lead us to believe?

_____

_____

_____

_____

_____

_____

Read Isaiah 55. How does God promise physical and spiritual nourishment to His people?

_____

_____

_____

_____

_____

_____

_____

_____

Practically, how can we invite others in for help when we find ourselves unmotivated to seek physical and spiritual nourishment? How can we practically meet this need for others?

_____

_____

_____

_____

_____

_____

week one
memory
verse

–

FOR I CONSIDER THAT
THE SUFFERINGS OF THIS
PRESENT TIME ARE NOT
WORTH COMPARING WITH
THE GLORY THAT IS GOING
TO BE REVEALED TO US.

–

ROMANS 8:18

week one
reflection

Write a brief summary of this week's passages.

_____

_____

_____

_____

_____

_____

_____

_____

What did you observe about God and His character from these passages?

_____

_____

_____

_____

_____

What do these passages teach you about the condition of mankind and about yourself?

_____

_____

_____

_____

_____

How do these passages point to the gospel?

How should you respond to these passages? What is the personal application?

What specific action steps can you take this week to apply these passages?

SHE KNEW THAT GOD WAS
SOVEREIGN EVEN OVER SUFFERING,
SO RATHER THAN PUSH HIM AWAY,
SHE SOUGHT HIM OUT.

hannah's story

Read: 1 Samuel 1

Year after year, Hannah's arms were still empty. Elkanah kept saying it did not matter because his love for her was strong even though she had never given him a child. But this was about more than pleasing her husband. Giving birth to a child was part of the design God had given her body as a woman, and the barrenness felt like a shameful statement about her identity. In addition to these dark thoughts filling her mind, Hannah was barraged regularly by her husband's second wife. Whenever the family took their annual journey to Shiloh for worship and sacrifice, Peninnah would berate Hannah with mocking words and taunting jeers along the way. To sour the pot even more, Hannah probably felt a great deal of social shame because her ability to contribute to society was severely diminished as a barren woman in Old Testament culture. All of these factors made up the circumstances leading to Hannah's depression.

Hannah's life had become one filled with bitter weeping, a lack of interest in things that should bring joy, a loss of appetite, deep distress, a troubled spirit, anxiety, vexation, and a broken heart. Though circumstantial, her battle with depression was by no means short-lived. At the point in time when we enter into her story in 1 Samuel 1, Hannah had likely been struggling this way for ten years or more.

As painful as it probably was to do so, Hannah appears to have continually brought this longing before the Lord in prayer through those long years. To whom else could she go? She knew that God was sovereign even over suffering, so rather than push Him away, she sought Him out. If anyone could open her womb or comfort her heart, it was the Lord God Almighty. And when He did not give her a baby, He was still the one to whom she could pour out her heart (1 Samuel 1:15). The portion of her prayer that we hear is filled with petitions and a vow. The intensity of her crying and silent prayer this particular day made Eli the priest think that she was drunk. But she explained to him that her heart was troubled and that she had been laying her anxieties and resentment before God. The Hebrew word that is translated as resentment in some translations here can also mean annoyance. So while Hannah had been making vows and sacrifices to the Lord, the substance of her prayer was honesty and wrestling. There was no pretense as she humbly emptied the genuine contents of her heart before the Lord.

Depression over circumstances in our lives can lead us to approach the Lord strictly with prayers seeking to persuade Him into changing our lot, if we even pray at all. We think we can hide our true feelings from the Lord when in reality He knows all our thoughts before we think them (Psalm 139:4). Maybe we pray prayers feigning a tone of contentment because we think if we can convince God that we are content with what He has given, then He will give us what we want. But the truth is that God is far more complex and infinitely more kind and understanding than this. When the apostle Paul talks about contentment in all circumstances in Philippians 4, he is not suggesting that we ignore our longings or delight in our brokenness; he is trying to communicate that we have joy outside of those changeable things, one that is permanent. God never asks us to pretend that the challenging or discouraging realities contributing to our depression are enjoyable. There is truly a great deal about our current condition that not even the Lord is content with and that He grieves over with us. Why would He ask you to be pleased with heartaches when the goal of His work through Christ has been to extinguish every one of them? The depression that you face is what Jesus died to end, and He wants to comfort you in the midst of it, not shame you out of it. But the truth is that our joy was never designed to be fed by our circumstances; it is meant to be fueled by Christ.

We are all waiting, like Hannah. Sometimes our waiting looks like hers — or maybe it is the wait for a spouse, a home, physical healing, relational restoration, or just for sadness to cease. But the heartbeat of all these longings is the cry of an even greater need. Every one of our unmet desires points to the fulfillment that only heaven and God's eternal presence can bring. Sometimes the Lord allows us to experience a tiny taste of that final satisfaction through earthly gifts. But even those who experience these earthly gifts may struggle with depression too. The gifts are not the answer; on earth, they will always be insufficient to satisfy the deepest longings of your heart. The giver of those gifts is your only real hope.

Likely, if you are reading this study, your battle with depression has not yet come to an end, or you long to see the end of a loved one's battle with similar circumstances. Because of this, it may have been challenging to read the end of 1 Samuel 1 and find out that Hannah's grief gave way to happiness and that her longing was met temporarily. But if you read closely, you will see that her depression lifted before her circumstances changed. It was after hearing a word from the Lord through the mouth of the priest that Hannah's countenance improved and her appetite returned. She had not seen the end of waiting yet, but God's Word was a comfort to her. The beauty of the Word of God is that it always tells the truth in ways that our emotions may not, and it is soul-satisfying in ways that nothing on earth is.

God's Word is not a consolation prize or a placeholder; it is a living and active comfort and help (Hebrews 4:12). Hannah recognized the power in the words of God, and she clung to them as a sufficient anchor for her heart, confident in God's promise to fulfill her desires. It was not that Hannah had the power to hold onto the words, but the Lord spoke to and soothed her heart through them. You have the same promise that Hannah had as you fight depression today. No, God has not promised to fulfill every earthly desire you have, but He has promised to satisfy your heart more fully in heaven than you could ever comprehend (Psalm 16:11). In the meantime, He has promised to be with you. And His Word is designed to anchor you through every hour of this challenging life. Read it when you do not feel like it, meditate on it, memorize it, pray it, recite it to yourself, and allow God's words to you to saturate your heart. He will meet you there and minister to your weary heart. You may not witness the end of your sorrow until heaven, but the God of all comfort will be with you in it.

"OUR JOY WAS NEVER DESIGNED TO BE FED BY OUR CIRCUMSTANCES; IT IS MEANT TO BE FUELED BY CHRIST."

Scripture is filled with descriptions of what God's Word is like. Read the following passages, and list the descriptions that God's Word gives about itself:

Isaiah 55:11 _____

_____

Psalm 33:6 _____

_____

Matthew 4:4 _____

_____

James 1:23 _____

_____

Psalm 119:105 _____

_____

Psalm 33:11 _____

_____

John 17:17 _____

_____

What do you feel like you are waiting for in life right now—change of circumstances, the fulfillment of specific desires, answers, hope?

_____

_____

_____

_____

_____

_____

_____

_____

_____

Read Revelation 21:1-6. How will the waiting you described in your previous answer be finished in heaven?

"THE BEAUTY OF THE WORD OF GOD IS
THAT IT ALWAYS TELLS THE TRUTH IN
WAYS THAT OUR EMOTIONS MAY NOT,
AND IT IS SOUL-SATISFYING IN WAYS
THAT NOTHING ON EARTH IS."

THE WAY WE PERCEIVE OUR
SITUATION INFLUENCES THE
WAY WE PERCEIVE OURSELVES.

naomi's story

Read: Ruth 1–4

Naomi's story begins with tragedy. Because of famine in Judah, she must leave her home and her people to move to Moab, a land filled with people who have fiercely rejected the Lord and instead chosen to serve false gods. Then, while in the foreign land, Naomi's husband dies. Her sons marry Moabite women, bringing even more disgrace on this Judaean family. Ten years into this real-life nightmare, Naomi's sons pass away, leaving her a childless widow with no family nearby to help as she has been dwelling in a foreign land all this time. Without friends or family around, Naomi is forced to make the journey back to Judah. She has heard that the Lord has blessed His people with prosperity anew there.

To Naomi, it seemed that the Lord was always blessing the people wherever she was not and that curses just followed her around. So as she enters Judah again after those many years of hardship, she has given herself a new name. Having felt pursued by affliction all her life, she refuses to be called Naomi anymore, which is a name that means pleasant or sweet. Naomi's life seemed anything but sweet, and so she tells the people of the town to address her as Mara, which means bitter. Naomi believed that God was sovereign, which meant that He had been in control of all the calamity that had come upon her. The grief had been so consuming that Naomi could only see herself in light of the affliction she had experienced. The grave events of her life were not just things that had happened to her; now she had taken their bitter substance on as her new identity.

As we grapple with various sorrows, it is our human inclination to seek our identity in those things. We may not even recognize it, but when we say things like, "I am depressed," we are no longer communicating a struggle we have, but we are redefining our identity based on that struggle. Naomi faced bitter events in her life, and she may have even battled the resulting bitterness in her own heart, but Naomi's true identity was not derived from the substance of her earthly experiences, and neither is ours. What we tack onto the words, "I am...," says a great deal about how we define ourselves. "I am bitter," or "I am depressed," are statements about identity, and they give our temporal struggles too much power over us.

The way we perceive our situation influences the way we perceive ourselves. God's perception is very different from ours, not only because He sees all but also because He always sees rightly. If we know Christ, God sees us as clothed in Christ's righteousness. We are Christians who wrestle with the lingering effects of sin and its sickness in a fallen world, but we are not defined by our sin or brokenness anymore. In Galatians 2:20, the Apostle Paul says that as Christians, we have been crucified with Christ, and His life is the one that defines our existence now, not our own. This does not mean that all that we are is negated or destroyed. God delights in us as His creation, and He designed us with beautiful intentionality. But it does mean that the former defining factor of sin in our lives has been so finally removed from us that Christ's work, power, and Spirit completely take its place, giving us a new identity. So, you may be a Christian struggling with depression, but you are no longer defined by that lingering element of the fall. You are defined as one who belongs to Christ and whose life is marked by the redeeming work that He is carrying out in you, even in this sorrowful struggle. This is how God sees us even when we choose to self-identify with our pain.

There is another difference in God's perception from which we need to glean when looking at ourselves from our limited viewpoints. Because God sees everything going on in and outside of our lives and is in control of all things, He is never worried or discouraged by the events that take place in our lives. All things work according to His plan. Even a battle with depression is not misplaced from His point of view. He uses all of the broken pieces in the world to construct the masterpiece of history that shapes into a work of art reflecting His glory. Yes, even your struggle with depression is something that God will use for His glory, though you may never fully understand how He does so. Consider Naomi—from her perspective, the theme of her life had been difficulty and distress. The sorrow of death and the burden of providing for herself would have felt insurmountable. It must have been challenging to even step out of bed each day and face the reality of her desolation anew.

But what Naomi could not see and may never have fully understood until she went home to be with the Lord in heaven was that none of her grief had been a strike from God's hand against her. Every loss had been a means of gain for God's eternal kingdom. The famine in Judah that led them to Moab and her sons' marriages to these Moabite women likely seemed like failures in light of the commands God had given Israel about not joining the other nations in their godless pursuits. But when her husband and sons died and Naomi returned to Judah, one of her daughters-in-law, Ruth, journeyed with her and found a spouse from Naomi's family lineage. Through those initially faulty marriages, the Lord was providing Naomi with comfort and a friend amidst the hardship—someone to care for her. But even more than that, He was knitting another nation into the clan of Judah and the family of God by Ruth's marriage to Boaz.

If you read the end of the book of Ruth, you found a lineage there. This may seem irrelevant or oddly placed, but it is a wonderfully relevant sign of future hope. From this lineage that included non-Jewish Ruth, the Savior, Jesus, would come. All of the grief that led to Naomi's depression was an instrument in God's good hands to provide an eternal home for her and all the nations of the world. This inclusion of a Moabite in the lineage of Christ is a foreshadowing of the mystery explained in Ephesians 3:6, which

reveals that ethnic Israel is not the only people whom Jesus died to deliver. We have to remember, and help others to remember, that the suffering—even the depression—that we face on this earth is never wasted by our kind, heavenly Father; He redeems it all for His glory and our eternal good. The tears we cry in the hours of this life will reap a harvest of glory to the Lord for eternity. Our finite perspective of pain never tells the whole, magnificent, redemptive story.

"HE USES ALL OF THE BROKEN PIECES IN THE WORLD TO CONSTRUCT THE MASTERPIECE OF HISTORY THAT SHAPES INTO A WORK OF ART REFLECTING HIS GLORY."

Read Psalm 126. How might the psalmist's words be a comfort and hope to you or someone you know who is wrestling with depression?

_____

_____

_____

_____

_____

_____

_____

Read Galatians 2:20. Why is the identity that Christ gives us better than the identity we take from our pain?

_____

_____

_____

_____

_____

_____

_____

_____

_____

Were there aspects of today's study that were challenging for you to read or believe? Take a piece of paper, and on one side, write the things that you found hard to believe. Then on the other side of the page, write out what you know to be true about each of those things, even if you do not feel like they are true today. You may also use the space provided on the next page to complete this exercise.

THINGS I FIND HARD TO BELIEVE:

_____
_____
_____
_____
_____
_____
_____
_____
_____
_____

WHAT I KNOW TO BE TRUE:

_____
_____
_____
_____
_____
_____
_____
_____
_____
_____

THE BEAUTY OF THE GOSPEL IS THAT
IT TRANSFORMS OUR UNDERSTANDING
OF PRESENT CIRCUMSTANCES AND
DIRECTS OUR FOCUS TO A JOY THAT
NEVER DIMINISHES OR FADES.

week 2 | *day 3*

job questions his life

Read: Job 1 & 3

We are first introduced to Job in the Scriptures as an exceedingly righteous man. We are given an impressive description of a man who was not perfect but who was certainly devoted and faithful to God. In a culture where wealth and distinction were considerably attached to the size of one's family, Job was greatly blessed. He had seven sons and three daughters whom it seems he cared for and shepherded well. Job 1:3 tells us that "His estate included seven thousand sheep and goats, three thousand camels, five hundred yokes of oxen, five hundred female donkeys, and a very large number of servants." He was a man of prominence and affluence in his community, easily admired and respected by others. By every indication, the Scriptures relays the depiction of Job as being "the greatest man among all the people of the east" (Job 1:3).

The life of Job is a considerable example of depression among men and women of faith. Though the opening introduction of the book of Job presented a man who seemingly had it all, it was soon all taken away from him. Satan entered into the picture and approached God to challenge and test the faithfulness of Job. He asserted that Job would not remain obedient to God without all of his life's wealth, happiness, and esteem. So God allowed Satan to test Job, and this led to a series of grievous losses in Job's life. Job experienced the loss of his worldly possessions, the loss of his sons and daughters, and an onslaught of physical ailments. Such loss in life would be difficult for anyone to endure, yet Job never sinned against God. By proclaiming truth over his circumstances, he battled the lie that tempted him to doubt God: "Naked I came from my mother's womb, and naked I will leave this life. The Lord gives, and the Lord takes away. Blessed be the name of the Lord" (Job 1:21).

Nevertheless, this does not negate that he struggled deeply with what was happening to him. He was grieved by his losses and was in emotional distress. In chapter 3, we find a flood of despair as he reaches his tipping point, cursing the day he was born and feeling it would have been better to never have been born. Job wondered why God would allow him to live if this was to be the content of his life. Questioning his life and his purpose, he plunged into self-pity and feelings of worthlessness. For any struggling through depression, this sentiment may sound familiar—questioning self and surroundings, wondering what the point of everything is. We can find ourselves in the same emotional and physical state as Job who cries out, "I sigh when food is put before me, and my groans pour out like water. For the thing I feared has overtaken me, and what I dreaded has happened to me. I cannot relax or be calm; I have no rest, for turmoil has come" (Job 3:24-26).

Job's circumstances provoked his depression. Loss, grief, trauma, misfortune, pain, and suffering—each of these things bears a crushing weight on anyone who experiences them. Such weight can sometimes lead to seasons of depression as we aim to uphold the weight in our human weakness and frailties. But Job's depression was also encouraged by his inward interpretation of his suffering. He began to question whether God was for him or against him and struggled to see the purpose and presence of God amid his pain. Job's example helps remind us that we are not the author of our circumstances. There will be moments or seasons in life that come upon us like a tidal wave—loss of loved ones or substantial material possessions, witnessing or experiencing traumatic events and life-threatening illnesses; the list could go on. Our natural response in this fallen world is usually grief, anger, or pain—sometimes all of these at once. Depression is the result of a broken world screaming for restoration and redemption. However, for Christians, we are not left in this brokenness. Jesus Christ has purchased peace for us through His life, death, and resurrection which pierces through the turmoil and points us to an everlasting hope in Him. The beauty of the gospel is that it transforms our understanding of present circumstances and directs our focus to a joy that never diminishes or fades—a joy that can withstand any trial, temptation, doubt, or fear and sustain us through even the most difficult times. We can interpret our circumstances, not by what is seen but by looking toward future glory.

As we continue delving into the life and experience of Job, we find that though he wrestled with depression, he ultimately kept his faith in God through all that happened. He believed God to be the sovereign, almighty, and wise Creator in control of all things, even those things he did not understand. Job held fast to who God said He was, even when he could not see it clearly for himself. As we walk through our own seasons of despair or endure them alongside friends or family, may we fight lies that aim to contradict the presence and purpose of God. May we, like Job, cling to the counsel of God's Word and pray for revelation from God. In the conclusion of the final chapter, Job claims, "I know that you can do anything and no plan of yours can be thwarted. You asked, 'Who is this who conceals my counsel with ignorance?' Surely I spoke about things I did not understand, things too wondrous for me to know" (Job 42:2-3).

"DEPRESSION IS THE RESULT OF A BROKEN WORLD SCREAMING FOR RESTORATION AND REDEMPTION."

How do you see the tension in the story of Job as one who trusts in the Lord and yet continues to battle depression? In what way do you resonate with this response?

_____

_____

_____

_____

_____

_____

The events of Job's life are tragic. Many circumstances in life will attempt to steal our joy and test our faithfulness to God. In what ways have you found those temptations to be true in your own life?

_____

_____

_____

_____

_____

_____

Read 1 Peter 1:6-9. How does God's Word point us toward a lasting joy in Christ that sustains us through the most unimaginable things? In what ways can you claim joy today?

_____

_____

_____

_____

_____

_____

WE CANNOT PRETEND TO SPEAK INTO
ANOTHER PERSON'S SITUATION WITH
COMPLETE UNDERSTANDING UNLESS WE
ARE THAT PERSON OR GOD HIMSELF.

job: the unhelpful words of friends

Read: Job 16

Have you been the recipient of unhelpful words? Most of us have been the recipient of unhelpful words at some point. Maybe it was your boss, a misguided professor, your spouse, or your closest friend. Or maybe it was a coworker, a well-meaning church friend, or just a random acquaintance. But it is possible that someone looked at your struggle with depression and responded with words that stung instead of soothed. Perhaps they chided, mocked, misunderstood, preached, accused, trivialized, minimized, or belittled. They meant the best, but the platitudes they shared only left you feeling more empty. When they took the time to listen and comfort, they may have expected that to be the end of your grief, but it was just the beginning of your journey. The next time you met, maybe they were surprised to hear that you were still not better. When they prayed over you, perhaps it felt accusatory and instructive and only left you feeling ashamed for your struggle with sadness. You did not think it was a sin to feel this weight, and you were right.

Job, of all people, was familiar with the insensitivity of even dear friends amid grief. His friends began well. They followed the cultural practice of silent co-mourning in keeping with a loss as great as the one Job had experienced. They waited for Job to speak first, which was also traditional in this setting. They waited seven whole days, which proved not to be long enough. As with most of us, their sensitivity and tact vanished the moment they opened their mouths. From Job's three friends came accusations of sin and twisted pieces of advice that they thought would remedy Job's situation. Their words accused Job of secret sins that must have been the cause of his depression. They questioned his faith, his actions, and even his degree of grief. So damaging were their words that Job did not know whether to speak or to be silent: "If I speak, my suffering is not relieved, and if I hold back, does any of it leave me?" (Job 16:6). Maybe with well-meaning intentions, these "miserable comforters," as Job calls them, run the gamut of hurtful responses to a person's pain.

The truth is that we cannot pretend to speak into another person's situation with complete understanding unless we are that person or God Himself. It is tempting to think, as Job's friends seemed to, that we can fix the problems our hurting friends are dealing with or that we have the power to speak words that will magically make the pain go away. You may think that if you were in their shoes, you would be able to shake it off and move on. Maybe you do not understand why they are so sad. If you feel this way in any sense toward a friend who is grieving loss or battling depression, then I encourage you to learn how to listen and to be patient in doing so. Listen even when your friend has no words to say. Listen when he or she shares problems that you think you can fix with your words. Listen when that person tells of grief that you do not understand. And before you ever speak, pray. Then question your motives in speaking, and pray again. Job's friends looked straight past him in all their speaking to him; they missed him entirely. Do not miss your friends in their hurt, but instead pray that God would give you words to speak that bring relief rather than adding to their grief.

For you who are battling depression and have borne the uninformed, callous comments of friends in and about your pain, take heart. Maybe when someone attempted to share Scripture with you in an inappropriate time or in an inappropriate way it hardened your heart toward God's Word or felt like a bandaid for a gushing wound. It may be tempting to let those misuses color your view of Scripture. It might feel like accusatory promises that you do not know how to believe, but the reality is that those promises are true whether or not you feel strong enough to believe them. God's Word is a living text, which means that its words are not ancient, irrelevant writings. They have power as the direct words of God written for your benefit and encouragement. Scripture does not get its power from you, but it is God's gift to you, and it works in you and your heart through His unfailing power.

Some friends will be intentionally unkind; others may mean to help but just do not know how. Learn to discern the difference, and then tell the true friends what you need from them. If you do not know, just ask them to read Scripture to you; maybe have them read through Psalms, Romans, or Philippians. Regardless of how your friends or others may respond to your struggle with depression, do not allow their often skewed voices to be the ones defining your relationship with the Lord. Job was derided probably more than you or I will ever be for our depression, and yet he says in the midst of it, "My friends scoff at me as I weep before God" (Job 16:20). Job knew that His advocate was in heaven and that no matter what his friends told him or how far God felt from him, it was to the Lord that he continually returned. He spoke to the Lord, grieved before Him, and wept to Him. Job was not a sinless man like Jesus, so he naturally made some mistakes in his speech throughout the book, but he prayed honestly and the Lord heard, answered, and restored him.

If you are in Jesus, the Lord will restore you too. It may not happen in the time frame that you anticipate or in the way that you have prayed, and it may not come as soon as your well-intentioned friends tell you that it will. But as you wait and wrestle, your struggle with depression is not sinful and neither was Job's. But like Job, you are a sinner, and you will sin in the midst of your depression, just as you would if you were not in a season of depression. If friends confront you for sin, weigh their words, ask the Lord if they are true, and examine your heart. You need repentance and grace just as much now as you did before. Drink deeply of repentance and the free mercy that God offers through Jesus to you. And remember, if friends falsely accuse you of sin, our advocate is in the heavens, and He sees and knows. His opinion is the only one that matters.

Read Hebrews 4:12. Why is it good that God's Word is powerful apart from our strength?

Read the following passages: Psalm 103:6-14, 1 John 1:9-2:2, Colossians 2:13-15. What do these tell you about God's attitude toward you in your sin?

God is your advocate against your sin and your sadness. How can this knowledge comfort you when friends speak hurtful words to you about those two things?

OUR SINFUL BODIES WANT TO
SIN, BUT GOD'S SPIRIT IN US
MAKES US WANT HIS HOLY WILL.

david's
story

Read: 2 Samuel 11 & 12

David is a man whose life is near to bursting with loss and grief. He was chased by a king, torn from the side of his dearest friend, watched his infant die, was betrayed by his son, and then forced to grieve the death of that son soon after. And yet in all of this, some of David's most profound grief came after his failed fights against his own sin. He was a king and one favored by the Lord, and yet sin had ruined his life — a faithful one whose life is a reminder that none of us are immune to sin. As the Psalms show, David wrote powerful songs of confession over specific sins he had committed. In them, the Lord has given us a model of true confession and genuine repentance over our sins, as we will see next week.

Our sin can be overwhelming and can even leave us feeling defeated at times. We fall into the same sins over and over, seemingly unable to stop making the same mistakes. We do things we do not want to do and yet feel incapable of doing what we know is right. This is the ever-present battle for every believer, as the Apostle Paul explains in Romans 7:15-20. There is a war continually waging within us between our fallen flesh and the gift of God's Spirit. Our sinful bodies want to sin, but God's Spirit in us makes us want His holy will. Outside of habitual sins, there may also be monumental sins in our past looming heavily in our definition of ourselves. Those failures in our past haunt us, just like David's did.

One of David's most well-known sins was his act of adultery with Bathsheba followed by his murder of her husband, Uriah. There were no excuses and no way to justify his actions. King David saw Bathsheba bathing on the roof one morning, and what his eyes saw, his heart soon demanded. This whole event speaks shame for David, because as the chapter begins, this was the time when kings were to go out to war, and Israel was in the middle of one of her worst. The ark of the covenant, an important symbol of God's power and presence, had been stolen. But where was David? Not only had he begun to look lustfully at this woman, but his very circumstance was a result of sinfully shirking his kingly responsibilities.

Though he knew better, David committed adultery with Bathsheba, and she became pregnant. David must have thought that he could have her and avoid the consequences, but now she bore his child. His failure was exposed. To cover sin, David committed more. He ordered his officers to murder righteous Uriah who had been away from home at war for the sake of the king and Israel—where David should have been. As you read 2 Samuel 11 and 12, you can almost feel the panic in David's heart. He had to cover his tracks, and in a skewed sense, he seemed to think he was making things right. In whose eyes? All that seemed to rule him were greed and selfishness. He disregarded the woman, her husband, and even indirectly, his own child. But in all this, David appears utterly blind to his actions and the reality of who his sins were really against–God.

Shortly after, God sent the prophet Nathan to open David's eyes to his sin. This was not the Lord taunting David for his mistakes, but God knew that David had been ignorant of his guilt, and so He mercifully sent Nathan to intervene. The Lord's sending of Nathan was a gentle way of drawing David into acknowledgment and repentance over his sin. Here we catch a glimpse of the Lord's heart toward us in our sin. Yes, our sins are vile—they deserve the just wrath of our holy God. But the Lord continually demonstrates Himself as a merciful father who is slow to anger and abounding in patient and consistent love. He covers and forgives those who trust in Him, and He did just that for shame-filled David.

This is how the Lord looks at you in your sin if you are in Jesus. Contrast this with how you may view yourself. Is there sin in your past that feels so great that you define your identity by it? No matter how terrible it may be, Christ's blood is sufficient to cover it. There is no sin He cannot forgive, and there is nothing He has not forgiven you for if you have come to Jesus in faith and repentance. The sin in your past does not define who God has remade you to be in His Son, Jesus. David sinned in terrible ways, and yet the Lord pursued his heart, loved him deeply, and used him for great purposes. It was never about David's ability to be righteous—it was always about God's ability to do righteous work through monumentally sinful and broken vessels like David, you, and me.

But maybe you are not a Christian. Maybe you have never accepted Jesus as your Savior from sin. Maybe you even feel irredeemable. Your mistakes did not just affect you, but they hurt others just as David's mistakes did. How could you ever be forgiven, you wonder. This was likely how David felt too–irredeemable. His mistakes seemed too great. And yet before he ever turned to the Lord to ask for forgiveness, God came near to him to draw him to repentance and restoration. The Lord has done the same with us through Christ. He sent Jesus when we were in our waywardness and sin and far from ever acknowledging it. Stained beyond belief with lives wrecked by sin's footprints, Jesus came to turn our eyes to the truth of our need and of His plentiful and free supply of mercy. Will you trust Him, friend?

God knows that we are weak in the fight, just as He knew David's weakness and sent Nathan as a means to help David fight his sin. And when you are united to Christ, God gives you His Holy Spirit to help you battle sin. So if you feel irredeemable because of your sin or burdened beyond belief by its weight, go to Jesus. You will not be met with chiding remarks; instead, you will find comfort and the Lord's strength to help you fight.

Read Romans 5. For whom did Jesus die? How does this passage prove wrong the idea that our sin is too bad to be forgiven?

_____

_____

_____

_____

Write a sentence about what relation sin has to your identity.

_____

_____

_____

_____

If you are in Jesus, what defines your identity?

_____

_____

_____

_____

How have you witnessed the Lord's kindness in revealing your sin to you?

_____

_____

_____

_____

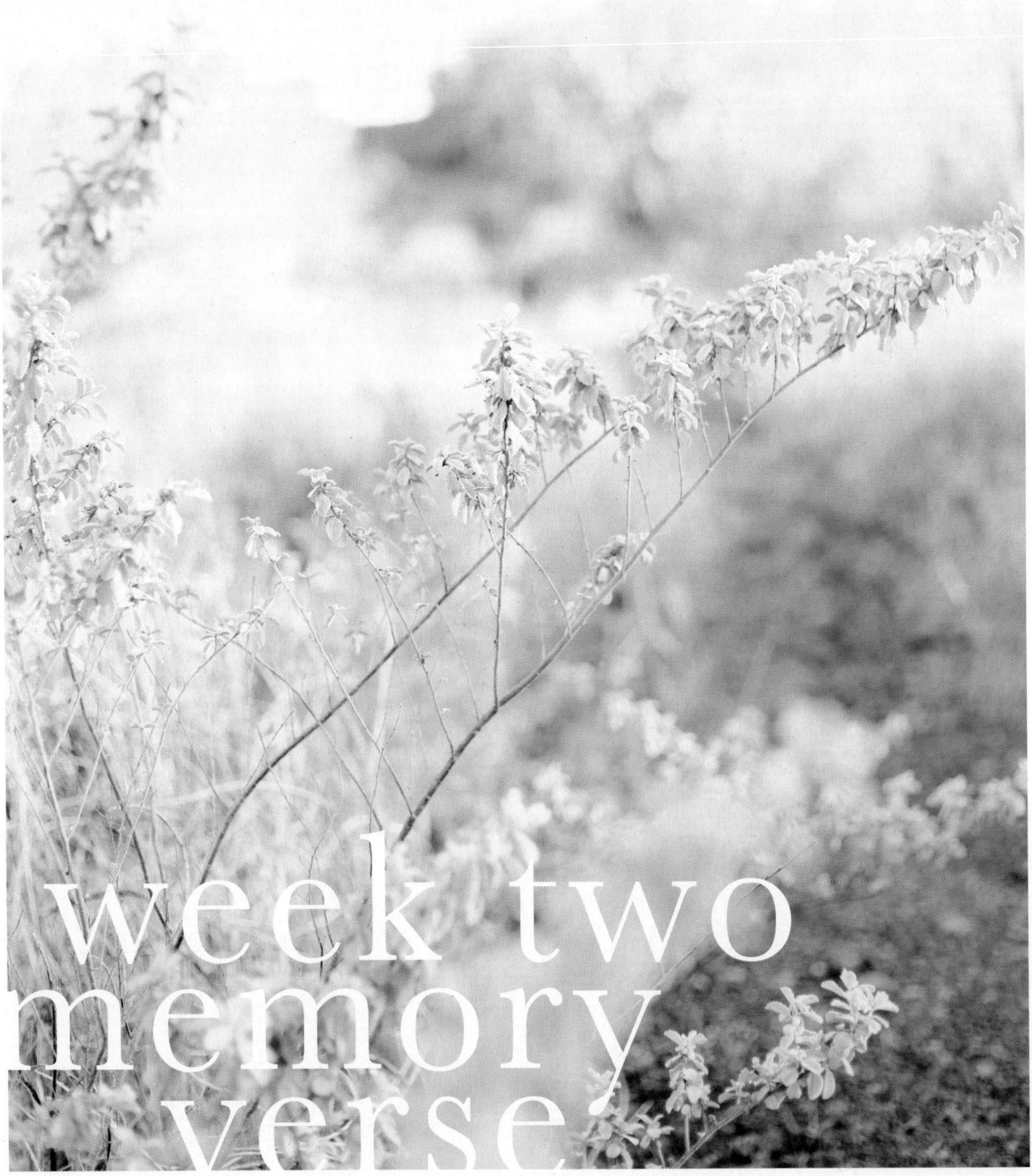

week two memory verse

—

FOR THE CREATION

EAGERLY WAITS WITH

ANTICIPATION FOR GOD'S

SONS TO BE REVEALED.

—

ROMANS 8:19

week two
reflection

Write a brief summary of this week's passages.

_____

_____

_____

_____

_____

_____

_____

What did you observe about God and His character from these passages?

_____

_____

_____

_____

What do these passages teach you about the condition of mankind and about yourself?

_____

_____

_____

_____

How do these passages point to the gospel?

How should you respond to these passages? What is the personal application?

What specific action steps can you take this week to apply these passages?

WHAT DAVID NEEDS CAN ONLY
BE BESTOWED UPON HIM, AND
ALL HE HAS TO DO IS ASK.

david: sin and guilt

Read: Psalm 51

When Nathan came and spoke to him about his sin against Bathsheba, David was convicted and turned to write the words of Psalm 51. In it, he speaks of guilt that is constantly on his mind. He cannot stop thinking about his mistake. The beauty of this psalm is how David acknowledges the full weight of his sin against God and yet still pleads for mercy with confidence, speaking of his expectation of full forgiveness. His words are not just ones of confession, but he is so bold as to make a plea before the God against whom he has grievously sinned. David can do this because he has good theology. In other words, he believes true things about God.

The devil wants you to have bad theology. He wants to tell you lies about God and about how God views you. He wants you to think that you are too far gone in your sin. When we buy into his lies, they can lead us to great discouragement over the guilt of our sin. All depression has a spiritual component, and its impact is apparent when a poor theology of our sin is the cause of our depression. Maybe we have given in to the discouragement and view the sadness as a fitting self-punishment because of how filthy we are. Or maybe we feel that God is punishing us for our sin by afflicting us with depression. Both of these responses to our sin leave us in a spiral of self-condemnation and a debilitating inward focus, unable to see a hope outside of ourselves. And both of these responses reveal our theology—they show what we believe about God. They both reveal that we do not trust in God's merciful character or the power of His forgiveness.

David confronts both of these misconceptions in his psalm. He models a productive way to respond to the discouragement of guilt. He goes before God, breaking the cycle of inward-focused self-condemnation that the enemy wants us to live in. David acknowledges the fullness of his guilt before God, and doing so leads him not to despair but to request. He asks God to cleanse him comprehensively and intimately from this guilt. By confessing his sin to God, David moves out of that spiraling cycle of self-focus that only lends itself to discouragement.

Notice that David offers nothing to God in his requests for this all-inclusive forgiveness and cleansing. He makes it clear that God does not want physical offerings or any of David's good works right now. What David needs can only be bestowed upon him, and all he has to do is ask. The kind of change that David anticipates undergoing from this forgiveness is one that will cleanse him from sin, restore his joy, and lead him to worship. This does not mean that if we are experiencing depression then we have not fully experienced God's forgiveness. A brief perusal of David's psalms will show that he was at more than one moment deeply discouraged and afflicted by depression. As we can see, sin can have prolonged effects on us that can lead to seasons of depression lasting for more than a moment.

Apart from Christ, all people are enslaved in this bondage to sin. But if you know Jesus as your Savior, He has saved you from sin. Sin may still be present in your life, but it no longer has power over you and neither does the guilt that it brings. You can feel the full weight of your sin and also lay it at the feet of Jesus, accepting the complete forgiveness that He offers. Not only that, but the Lord will continually remake you as you come to Him with your sin. Because of your faith in Jesus, the Holy Spirit lives inside of you and is placed there to remind you of the truth and do the work of sanctification in your life. He is the one who gives us a new heart, a new will, and a restored conscience. This is why David pleads that the Holy Spirit might not be taken from him.

Maybe you are wondering how David experienced all of this before Christ came to earth and carried out His saving work. The truth is that God has always been in the business of forgiveness, and even Old Testament figures like David looked forward in hope and trust to the Messiah, Jesus, who would cover their sins by His future work. David's faith was ultimately faith in Christ, even though he never knew His name. Jesus has always been God's plan for salvation. In Him, God has blotted out all of David's transgression. The Holy Spirit was active in the hearts and lives of God's people then as well, though now He lives in us in a fuller and abiding way.

Experiencing God's forgiveness may not mean that depression immediately ceases. You can be a broken-hearted believer who still knows and can sing of the joy of your salvation from day-to-day in the throes of depression. But if guilt over sin is ever-present in your mind and feels like a weight over your life—a weight that steals your joy and speaks of despair that has led you into this depression—then there is sweet relief available to you, friend. The gifts of confession and repentance are yours, as they were David's. A heart that is broken over sin delights the Lord, but the brokenness was never meant to be the end of His plan. Seek the help of a wise friend, an elder, or your pastor, and ask that they help you work through the false ideas that have made their way into your theology. In the meantime, while you learn to form good theology, let psalms like this one move you through the motions of confession and acceptance of the forgiveness offered to you through Christ.

"A HEART THAT IS BROKEN OVER SIN DELIGHTS THE LORD."

Read Psalm 51 again. As you read, pray its words as a personal prayer.

List the ways mentioned in Psalm 51 that forgiveness and cleansing will lead David to actions of praise.

What do you have to rejoice in, even in your journey through depression?

THERE IS NOWHERE THAT YOU CAN
GO IN YOUR SADNESS, SIN, OR
SUFFERING THAT GOD HAS NOT
ALREADY FILLED WITH HIS PRESENCE.

God will meet us where we are

Read: Psalm 139

In Psalm 139, David speaks about the beauty of the all-knowing, ever-present God, perfect in supreme knowledge of all things and yet intimately near to His people. God's character is always a source of comfort for believers, and these two aspects of God's character are particularly encouraging for those who are walking through seasons or lives marked by depression. You may feel as if God is far off during your depression or does not know that it is happening to you—that if He does know, He is disappointed that you have found a home in this darkness and cannot approach you until you undo what you seem to have done to yourself. Listen close to this psalm. There is so much more for you than the lies you have heard in the darkness of this fight.

How startling must David's opening words have felt to you in this psalm! "Lord, you have searched me and known me," he says. The limits of God's knowledge regarding David are non-existent. The Lord knows not only intricate details about David's day to day life and actions, but God knows more about David than David knows himself. He knows David's thoughts before he even thinks them. God's knowledge is not a detached knowledge of His people, as David explains when he says that God has placed His very hand on him. God does not just know David—He knows him in a personal and purposeful way.

Not only is God knowledgeable about David's life and all things, but He is near to David. This awesome, holy, perfect-in-knowledge, divine One is near to this lowly, seemingly insignificant human. But David is not insignificant to the supreme God. He intentionally designed David's every physical, emotional, and spiritual facet in his mother's womb. There were no elements of David that God left to chance or natural processes. David's life has been the purposeful design of this sovereign God from day one on into eternity and at every step in between. God has designed your days in the same way—even these days that feel so dark.

God knows you intimately because His knowledge of your life is not gathered from a cosmic, impersonal perspective but through intimate involvement and purposeful design and care. God Himself is the one who formed you and your very days; He knows the sum of them because He fashioned them. He is both personal and sovereign. He is both near and knowing. He is over all things and yet intimately present. And in His nearness and knowledge, He is full of love for you through Christ. The Lord has never ceased pursuing you. From before your very conception, this Father God knew you in your entirety and was planning a life that would lead you into an eternity-long relationship with Himself, and He sacrificed His Son to accomplish that reality.

There is nowhere that you can go in your sadness, sin, or suffering that God has not already filled with His presence. There is nowhere you can flee that He will not run to meet you. He can do this because when you accepted Christ, He sent His Spirit into your heart. God is also near to you through His Word in the Bible, because it is there that He reveals Himself to you. If you try to pretend everything is okay and attempt to defy the darkness with a gutsy will-power, He is there. He is near and knowing how you really feel and what you really need. If you sink to the very depths of the earth, unable to rise from bed for days or weeks at a time because the darkness is too dim to even feel your way about, or because the weight is just far too heavy for you to lift, He is there right beside you, completely aware of your weakness. If you say that your very soul is darkness itself and that you just want to surrender to its grip because you are too tired to fight anymore, He has not left you, even in the lowest of pits. Not only is He there, but David also tells us in this psalm that even in those dark places, the Lord is our Light.

When we who belong to Jesus define ourselves by depression, the Lord is not fooled; He sees your real identity, and His thoughts of you are precious. He knows you in ways you do not and could not ever know yourself, because He knows of a future He has prepared for you that you cannot fathom, even on your best day. He knows of His strength that is holding you up and carrying you through, even on your very, very worst days, even when you cannot feel it. One of the most beautiful things about God is His eternal, stable character. He is not defined by our feelings. When He feels far away, we can preach to ourselves the reality that He is near because His Spirit lives in us through Jesus. When He feels detached from our world, we can remind ourselves of the truth that He sees and knows it all. And in seeing and knowing, He neither runs from nor scowls at our darkness, but He meets us in it with His Spirit and His Word. No matter how hard we try or how certain we are that we have done it, we cannot push God away in our depression. He will forever see us clothed in the blood of His perfect Son, and His abounding love for us, because of that reality, will cause Him in compassion to pursue us long into eternity.

God is never passive in this pursuit. He is active in His knowledge and is working in His nearness. David acknowledges this by his opening and closing words. He tells us at the beginning of the psalm that God has searched him and knows him, and at the end, he asks again that the Lord would continue to search and know him and then lead him into everlasting life. You can pray this too. God has searched you and knows you with and without this depression. He knows about the school work that has been left undone in this season. He knows about your grief over meeting your children's needs when you cannot get out of bed. He knows about the career that feels jeopardized because of this pit. He cares for you, your life, your children, your spouse, and your future far more than you do. Ask Him to search out the darkness with His light and lead you to Himself, day after day. Even if the depression never breaks on this earth, the sunrise will come, and you will wake in it, still with the Lord.

"EVEN IF THE DEPRESSION NEVER BREAKS ON THIS EARTH, THE SUNRISE WILL COME, AND YOU WILL WAKE IN IT, STILL WITH THE LORD."

Read the following passages about the Holy Spirit, and answer the questions below:
John 14:26, John 16:7-8, 13-15, 1 Corinthians 3:16, 1 Corinthians 2:10-11,
Ephesians 1:13-20.

Who is the Holy Spirit, and where does He live? _____

_____

_____

_____

What does He do? _____

_____

_____

_____

What is His power capable of accomplishing? _____

_____

_____

_____

If God knows all things, list some specific things He knows about you that no one else may know.

_____

_____

_____

_____

_____

_____

_____

_____

Does it surprise you that God knows everything about you and is still willingly and eagerly near to you? Why or why not?

_____

_____

_____

_____

_____

_____

"NO MATTER HOW HARD WE TRY OR HOW CERTAIN WE ARE THAT WE HAVE DONE IT, WE CANNOT PUSH GOD AWAY IN OUR DEPRESSION."

THE PSALMIST IS CONFIDENT THAT
THE LORD IS STILL THE GOD OF HIS
LIFE WHO WILL SHOW LOVE TO HIM
DAY AND NIGHT.

week 3 | day 3

instructing
our souls

Read: Psalm 42

Psalm 42 is one of the most encouraging and challenging psalms to read in the midst of depression. It can both sting and soothe all at once. We do not know for certain who wrote this psalm, but the instruction that the Psalms give for depression is unified, and we can see hope for the darkness throughout the book. Truly, all the psalms are a salve for the weary soul. The book of Psalms presents us with the reality of brokenness in the world through first-hand experience, but it moves through lament toward praise. These psalms are not stagnant in sorrow. Moving through the motions of praise as we read and pray them is so valuable for our souls, even when we cannot seem to feel it in depression.

Psalm 42 in particular was written from the heart of someone battling sorrow or even depression of some kind. The author is longing for the Lord in such desperation that he compares it to the feeling of being thirsty—a thirst like that of being dehydrated in the desert. His enemies taunt him about the Lord, and all the while the author is remembering how things used to be. He thinks of a time when he could feel the Lord's presence when he would be the one to lead others in worship of God. He remembers when he felt glad and was even joyful in his praise and his heart. But again, these things are a memory.

In verse 5, the author begins looking inward, questioning his own soul. He feels a sadness that he cannot explain and which has led him to feel numbness toward the Lord, yet he knows that in the past he was able to praise God. So he questions his soul, asking, "Why, my soul, are you so dejected? Why are you in such turmoil?" The author repeats later in the psalm as if he has yet to receive an answer. Each time he questions his soul, he also gives it an instruction: "Put your hope in God, for I will still praise him, my Savior and my God." Even though he is steeped in turmoil with a downcast heart, he commands and encourages his soul to trust in the Lord, knowing that even though he is not able to praise Him actively at this moment, he will praise Him again in the future. He questions how his soul could feel so hopeless when it knows of the surest hope of all—God. Why, soul, are you so troubled? Do you not know who your God is?

The author can be confident in his future ability to praise the Lord because of the Lord's faithful and steadfast character, of which the writer reminds himself starting in verse 6. The author says that he writes these words from the land of the Jordan, near the two mountains of Hermon and Mizar. This location would have been very far from the land of Jerusalem, the author's homeland. Jerusalem would also have been the location of the temple, the place where he used to worship. We do not know if the author was physically far from the temple at the time of this psalm, but regardless of his geographical location, the author feels far from the Lord's presence. Yet even in this deep depression, the psalmist is confident that the Lord is still the God of his life who will show love to him day and night. He knows that God's faithfulness toward him will never cease, even when he is in this darkness without any answers. So why, oh soul, are you so troubled? Remember who your God is.

Maybe in the confusion of your darkness, you have come before the Lord to ask similar questions the psalmist asks in verses 9-10. The striking thing about these questions and concerns that the writer brings before the Lord is the way he addresses the Lord as "God, my rock." It is okay to ask the Lord the tough questions and to even ask why it feels like He has forgotten us. But we must do so, like the psalmist, from this position of humility and a recognition of our dependence upon Him. God is our Rock, even when we come before Him with questions about how He feels far or seems as if He has forgotten us. Like the psalmist, we can ask the hard ques-

tions, but we must always come back to the truth that we can trust in God even when we have not yet received the answers to those questions, even when you do not know when the depression will end, even when you do not know why you no longer feel the spiritual strength and nearness you once felt, and even when you do not know when that strength will ever return. Even in this place, you can look to the Lord and His word, seeking Him through prayer, through the questions and the turmoil, confident that one day the end of the darkness and weakness will come and the light and strength will return. Oh soul, do you hear this? Do you see who your God is?

Sometimes what this confidence looks like, practically, is speaking to your soul just as the psalmist did. He asks the hard questions to God, his Rock, and yet always returns to the question, "Why, oh soul? Why are you so hopeless?" The psalmist is examining himself here. He wants to know why his soul refuses to be comforted by the reality of who he knows his God to be. You can ask yourself the same question when the sadness seems to come for no reason: Why, soul, are you so troubled? Do you know who your God is? Do you not know that you will praise Him again someday, forever? Because the truth is that if you are in Christ, you will praise God again. You may not feel like doing so now, but even if it is not until heaven, you will praise Him again. The joy will return, and in heaven, you will never lose it. Praising Him is what you were made for, and one day, you will do so again and never cease.

"PRAISING HIM IS WHAT YOU WERE MADE FOR."

After reading Psalm 42, what stands out to you? What comforts you?

In what ways do you resonate with the heart of the author's cry, "Why, my soul, are you so dejected? Why are you in such turmoil?" How have you personally wrestled with believing truths when your feelings do not match?

How can we position ourselves to hear the truths of God even when we do not feel like it? Why is this important?

WEEP AND PRAY AND GRIEVE AND PLEAD FOR GOD'S MERCY AND HIS INTERVENTION. BUT WHEN YOU ARE DONE, DRY YOUR TEARS, LIFT YOUR EYES, AND CLING TO CHRIST.

week 3 | day 4

jeremiah's story

In Jeremiah 8 and 9, and truly throughout this grieving prophet's book, we hear the strong voice of depression from Jeremiah's pen. The unique element of Jeremiah's sadness though is that it has little to do with himself. Depression can stem from an inward bent in our thinking, but for Jeremiah, the sorrow he experienced came from living in a world in which he was painfully aware of the darkness. Jeremiah was a prophet during the Old Testament period, which means he received messages directly from God, and it was his job to communicate those messages to the people around him. This meant that Jeremiah often went out publicly before crowds of people or even before the king and his officials to declare the new messages that he had received from the Lord.

Not all the prophets of the Old Testament had it quite as hard as Jeremiah, but he lived among a seriously stubborn and sinful people. His prophetic career was marked by grief, terror, and fear as he watched his people spiral further and further down into their sins. Not even one's own family members could be trusted, and oppression was rampant (Jeremiah 9:4-6). If those scenes were not grief-provoking enough, Jeremiah was also tasked with delivering God's messages of judgment against these treacherous people. The Lord was promising to bring destruction on the people of Israel if they did not repent of their sinful lifestyles and seek Him again. These people were engaged in every kind of sin—from sexual sins and slavery to child sacrifice and idol worship and every horror in between. The people of Israel were steeped in a season of actively pursuing sin instead of their good God. When Jeremiah tried to warn them about the destruction that would take place if they did not repent, they would mock and abuse him and often even try to physically harm him. This God-fearing, faithful man was deep in depression, largely because he knew and trusted the Lord.

Jeremiah knew and trusted God's words, and yet he battled deep depression. How could this be? Jeremiah was in direct contact with the Lord and was able to hear God's voice all the time. But the reality is that while Jeremiah knew the Lord and trusted His words, the words he heard from God spoke desolation for his home and the destruction of his people. Jeremiah lived among treacherous men and women who hated God and served only themselves. It was extremely challenging for Jeremiah to be a follower of God in his day. He loved God and was grieved for his people who would face judgment because they did not love or want to know God (Jeremiah 9:3, 6). And yet Jeremiah was also grieved by his people because of their sin and wickedness. Everywhere he turned, he saw the destruction of sin and a dim future for his people. It was because Jeremiah trusted God's words that he lived with this unceasing sorrow. He knew that when God promised to punish the people for their sins, He meant it.

Sadly, it does not take more than a few chapters of Jeremiah to remind us of our modern world and its brokenness. The darkness of sin and people's resistance to God's Word has been the theme of the ages throughout history. Truly, there is nothing new under the sun. But the sadness that comes with watching a sin-loving world usually strikes us in new and painful ways every day. The modern slave trade, the abortion industry, racial injustice, the hunger and famine across the globe, the violence on the streets and even in our homes, and a thousand other evils that are present in this world—no matter where we go on this earth, like Jeremiah, we cannot escape the reality of sin and brokenness. One of the hardest things about living in this world is watching people we love who are hurting in their slavery to sin but who refuse to accept the healing that Christ offers.

Jeremiah preached a weighty message: repent or perish. But there was hope in it. There was tremendous hope for those who would repent because they could then hope in the coming Messiah who would rescue them from their sin and the destruction it leads to. But as is often the case in our modern world, the people did not want to hear the message Jeremiah had from God. They did not care about the consequences, and they were far too stubborn to repent and take hold of the life offered to them in Jeremiah's words from God. That is why Jeremiah felt what seemed to him an overwhelming grief. The world he knew was falling apart while there was a remedy available. He was brokenhearted for their inevitable judgment and yet endlessly grieved by their evils. This tension should feel familiar to you too. We are constantly faced with sin and a world of people who push God away, their only hope for salvation and life. We grieve the future of our friends, family, and strangers while we also ache over the chaos and corruption that their sin reaps in daily life.

The brokenness in this world is all we need to feel the feelings of depression, and maybe your own heart is sick with this kind of grief. For Jeremiah, life moving forward looked like being faithful to proclaim God's message—the good parts and the hard parts—and learning to grieve over the brokenness of the people around him as it was rightfully grievous. His life was in constant tension between sadness and hope. That is the theme of our lives as believers on this earth. As we will see, even Jesus held this same tension in His heart when He walked the earth. So if sin and its consequences are breaking your heart and encouraging your sadness, do not be afraid to cry the tears and feel those feelings because this world is barren and dark, and there are many reasons to weep. Weep and pray and grieve and plead for God's mercy and His intervention. But when you are done, dry your tears, lift your eyes, and cling to Christ. Move from lament to praise as you thank God for the mercy that He has abundantly shown, through Jesus, to you and to so many others who do know Him. Thank Him for His plan to redeem all things and to destroy all evil. And even if the sadness still feels heavy on your chest, trust the Lord to carry you through it and be present in it as He works in mighty ways to redeem every broken piece of this world and your heart.

Read 1 Thessalonians 4:13-18. What do you hope in as you grieve?

_____

_____

_____

_____

_____

_____

Read Romans 8:18-30. Name some of the ways that you have witnessed creation groaning under the weight of sin.

_____

_____

_____

_____

_____

_____

_____

Who does Romans 8 say is our help as we wait for redemption? What does He do for us?

_____

_____

_____

_____

_____

_____

JEREMIAH'S GREATEST DANGER
WAS NOT HIS BATTLE WITH
DEPRESSION; HIS GREATEST
DANGER WAS FORGETTING GOD
IN THE MIDST OF IT ALL.

week 3 | day 5

jeremiah: the importance of remembering

Read: Lamentations 3:52-58, Jeremiah 38

Jeremiah divulged an emotion-filled response to his misfortune in Lamentations 3. He felt rejected and abandoned by God and devoid of any hope. He summarized his life by naming the physical pains, the unrelenting hardship, and the dark cloud that seemed all-consuming amidst his righteous efforts. The words that fill this chapter reflect Jeremiah's aching heart and depression. For those who, like Jeremiah, are battling depression, his words may put a name to your own feelings. They may resonate with recognition you wish you did not have to claim—finding yourself in overwhelming scenarios, searching for a glimpse of light, and easily enumerating each aspect of your life that has seemingly led you to this place. You may feel you have been given an impossible task. You may feel you do not have the strength or capacity to carry on. Like Jeremiah, you may feel completely alone in it all. The absence of those you love only exacerbates the pangs of hurt and sorrow you feel.

Jeremiah's life was one of great sacrifice. But his sacrifice was not well received or even understood by those closest to him. The mission and message entrusted to him by God came with extreme opposition. Ridiculed, rejected, and mocked by all, it may seem as if he could not possibly suffer or endure any longer. Soon enough, he found himself labeled a traitor for the message he proclaimed and thrown into a dungeon-like prison. Jeremiah 38:6 recounts, "So they took Jeremiah and dropped him into the cistern of Malchiah the king's son, which was in the guard's courtyard, lowering Jeremiah with ropes. There was no water in the cistern, only mud, and Jeremiah sank in the mud." Not only was he encircled with gloom, but he was also physically encapsulated in the darkness of a pit in the ground. Jeremiah found himself in the utmost place of despair. He tells us in Lamentations 3:52-54, "For no reason, my enemies hunted me like a bird. They smothered my life in a pit and threw stones on me. Water flooded over my head, and I thought, 'I am going to die!'"

If there had been an end of the rope, Jeremiah was there. Yet for God's people, there is always hope beyond the present—a hope we must pray to be reminded of time and time again. It is a hope we must fight for with every fiber of our being so that we do not lose sight of it. God does not abandon His people. Jeremiah continued His poetic remembrance: "I called on your name, Lord, from the depths of the pit. You heard my plea: Do not ignore my cry for relief. You came near whenever I called you; you said, 'Do not be afraid.' You championed my cause, Lord; you redeemed my life" (Lamentations 3:55-58). In his greatest moment of need, Jeremiah called out to the Lord in desperation, and God's response should not surprise us. He came near. God never abandoned Jeremiah, even when he felt most alone and hopeless. We are reminded of this through Jeremiah's proclamation of God's presence and nearness amidst his darkness.

A common posture the Scriptures present is that of remembering. After the great flood in Genesis, God made a covenant with Noah that He would never flood the earth again (Genesis 9:11). He placed a rainbow in the clouds as a covenant sign of remembrance so that Noah and all generations to come would remember God's mercy displayed and promise sustained. In Moses' final address to the Israelites before they crossed over to the Promised Land without him, he exhorts them to remember—to call to mind all the things they have seen so that they will not forget God's faithfulness to them and will teach it to generations to come (Deuteronomy 4:9). In the New Testament when Paul is writing to Timothy, one of his disciples, he encourages him to remember the death and resurrection of Jesus Christ (2 Timothy 2:8) so that he may stand firm on the truth of the gospel amidst opposition. As we see time and time again, we are prone to wander and forget. Remembering is a necessary practice for the Christian to remain faithful.

Jeremiah's greatest danger was not his battle with depression; his greatest danger was forgetting God in the midst of it all. The goodness and faithfulness of God pierces through even the deepest of pains and darkest of circumstances. For the Christian, God has equipped us with the Holy Spirit to guide and help our remembering, to bring to light the truths we have heard and known (John 14:26). He has gifted us with His Word, chronicling the stories of His faithfulness and instructing us on the way forward. And He has promised us His presence as sun and shield, withholding no good thing from those who walk uprightly (Psalm 84:11).

Remembering who God is and what He has done for His people brings us out of our present and pressing surroundings. This holds great impact when compounded with the misconceptions we may feel about Him amidst depression. Remembrance brings us to uncover the hope that may seemingly be hidden from us. When we call to mind the ways God has moved in our lives and the lives of others, we are inclined toward His character, His promises, and His eternal presence. When we consider the testimonies of God's faithfulness through the ages, we can remain hopeful for the ways God will use us to further reveal Himself to His people, even in their depression.

"REMEMBERING IS A NECESSARY PRACTICE FOR THE CHRISTIAN TO REMAIN FAITHFUL."

How might you resonate with the story of Jeremiah?

Jeremiah was enlisted with a difficult task which resulted in many abandoning him and leaving him alone. How does God continue to help and comfort us even when walking through seasons of isolation or lacking close relationships?

In what ways throughout Scripture do we see the effects of remembering who God is in the midst of trials? What are practical ways we can continually be reminded of who God is?

week three
memory
verse

-

FOR THE CREATION WAS
SUBJECTED TO FUTILITY—NOT
WILLINGLY, BUT BECAUSE OF HIM
WHO SUBJECTED IT—IN THE
HOPE THAT THE CREATION ITSELF
WILL ALSO BE SET FREE FROM THE
BONDAGE TO DECAY INTO
THE GLORIOUS FREEDOM
OF GOD'S CHILDREN.

-

ROMANS 8:20-21

week three
reflection

Write a brief summary of this week's passages.

_____
_____
_____
_____
_____
_____
_____
_____
_____

What did you observe about God and His character from these passages?

_____
_____
_____
_____
_____
_____

What do these passages teach you about the condition of mankind and about yourself?

_____
_____
_____
_____
_____
_____

How do these passages point to the gospel?

How should you respond to these passages? What is the personal application?

What specific action steps can you take this week to apply these passages?

JESUS REMAINED UNBLEMISHED BY SIN, UNDETERRED FROM HIS PLANS, AND FAITHFUL IN HIS OBEDIENCE TO THE FATHER.

week 4 | day 1

Jesus, our perfect example

Read: Isaiah 53

The Bible presents us with many stories serving to show what it looks like to faithfully walk through depression. But there is only One who provides a perfect example for us, and that person is Jesus Christ. His divinity did not exempt Him from living as we lived and seeing the world through the eyes of humanity. He had earthly parents, siblings, and friends. He did not possess a noteworthy appearance or impressive form. He was not given special privileges but lived as an ordinary man. He grew up in the world experiencing the lessons and growth of childhood. He grew into his teenage years, taking on responsibilities and learning to function in society. Maturing into an adult, Jesus remained unblemished by sin, undeterred from his plans, and faithful in His obedience to the Father. He dealt with the reality of living in a sinful and suffering world as a human. He was despised and rejected. He knew pain and disappointment. He knew sickness and death, and He walked through unspeakable sorrow.

Isaiah 53 refers to Jesus Christ as a man of sorrows acquainted with grief. The description of Christ given in this chapter does not feature an unapproachable Savior who is enthroned in the heavens and removed from the groans of the earth. It does not portray one who speaks words from which He cannot draw comfort and strength. Instead, this chapter unveils the earthly anguish Jesus finds all too familiar and how His response speaks into our deepest depression. Should we question His instruction to reorient our hearts back to the will and work of God amidst the circumstances we face, we must remember that Jesus Himself drew strength from doing so and endured faithfully to the end of His life on earth.

Jesus Christ's life paved a way for all who share in His suffering. Every step He asks us to take, He has not only walked before us but continually walks with us. He submitted to the will of the Father, trusting in His sovereignty and goodness, so we can submit to Christ. Though the outcomes may seem undesirable or even impossible to bear, we have the help of One who now stands on the other side. Jesus Christ defeated the grave, resurrected, and ascended to sit at the right hand of the Father. Through His sacrifice as the righteous servant, He will justify many and carry their iniquities (Isaiah 53:11).

Jesus willingly took on the sin and suffering of others to intercede on their behalf. He carried the sickness, sadness, rebellion, and grief of sinners. He wore the pains and scars of the broken. He loved and served with no restraint. He humbly embraced affliction so that others might be set free from it. He was punished, beaten, tortured, and eventually put to death. Can you imagine the physical and emotional turmoil He must have faced? Can you imagine the pain and punishment He endured? Can you imagine the weight Christ carried? Though the burden was tremendous, His purpose outweighed His oppression, and He endured faithfully to the end. He could have exempted Himself from every tear and trial, but He did not. He could have spared Himself from grief and death, but He did not. He carried His own cross where He would hang to be crucified, to carry God's people through the pangs of depression, through this life to the next.

Though we may find ourselves searching for the other side of our battle with depression, Jesus, like others represented in Scripture, did not find relief during His time on earth. Yet, His life ends in victory and triumph. He used His suffering to accomplish for us what no one else but Him could ever accomplish. He not only defeated sin that so relentlessly seeks to devour us, but He pur-chased a peace for His people that surpasses all understanding—a peace that is accessible to all who find their hope and healing in Jesus Christ, a peace that calls us to relinquish our grip on every affliction of this world and cast them on Christ, a peace that calls us out of this world to long for heaven and hope for eternal rest. When all that surrounds us tempts us to despair with seemingly no end in sight, may the life and example of Jesus Christ remind us that there is another way. May His purchased peace hold a candle to the darkness and bring us comfort and endurance until He brings us to our final rest in Him.

"JESUS CHRIST'S LIFE PAVED A WAY FOR ALL WHO SHARE IN HIS SUFFERING."

After reading Isaiah 53, list every word that describes Jesus' earthly affliction. How does this exemplify Him as a Man of Sorrows, acquainted with grief?

_____

_____

_____

_____

_____

_____

_____

In what ways does Jesus' example of suffering change the way you approach Him in your suffering?

_____

_____

_____

_____

_____

_____

What hope and comfort do you find in the peace purchased for us through Jesus' suffering? In Christ, how can you claim peace that surpasses all understanding today?

_____

_____

_____

_____

_____

_____

JESUS CAME WITH REDEMPTION
AND COMFORT.

where were you, Lord?

Read: John 11:1-44

Maybe throughout the study, you have had moments of feeling torn or even confused between the themes of hope for the future and the reality of your present situation. You hear so much talk of future healing and hope, and yet you wonder why those realities cannot all be part of the present. Why is God not using His power to prevent the pain you feel now? If He has the power to repair it, why is He waiting so long to heal the brokenness? The depression is present and heavy, and you are confident that God has the power to protect you from it. Yet here you are.

Mary and Martha posed similar questions for Jesus when He showed up four days after their brother, Lazarus, had died. They had sent for Jesus when Lazarus was sick, certain He would come. Jesus loved Lazarus, so why would He not come and heal him? And yet here they were, four days into the heart-sickening grief that death brings. Their hearts were still confident in Jesus' power but confused at His purposes. They knew that if Jesus had been there, their brother would not have died. But Jesus had not been there. Death seemed to have won again, and the sisters were sick with confusion as they told Jesus how He could have saved their brother. You can almost hear the heaviness of their hearts as you read their repeated mantra, "Lord, if you had been here, my brother wouldn't have died." Behind this statement are the questions: Lord why were you not here? Lord, where were you?

The narrative leading up to when Jesus finally came to visit them reveals that Jesus neither forgot about Lazarus nor did He misjudge his timing. Jesus' actions are calculated according to His specific intention. He wanted to arrive after Lazarus had died. Why? Why would Jesus want His loved ones to experience this pain? The people who came to grieve with the family and see Jesus arrive and weep over the lifeless man ask similar questions. Some of them asked, "Couldn't he who opened the blind mans' eyes also have kept this man from dying?"

Of course, if you read the end of the passage, you know that Jesus raised Lazarus from the dead. Often when we hear this story from Scripture, that resurrection moment is the focal point for good reason, but we cannot miss that so much takes place before redemption. What we often forget is that Jesus spent the majority of this particular passage experiencing the broken reality of a fallen world along with the people who lived with its pain day after day. He did not pass over the very real heartache they felt. It is here in these moments of grief that we want to focus on today because, in our current point in history, this place between sorrow and redemption is where we live.

The reality of sin in the world means that everything is fractured—even good things. Nothing in this world is yet as it should be. Jesus entered into this reality when He came to earth, and He did not wave a wand to make it all disappear in a moment, because the past and present pain were real, and we see Him acknowledging its reality with compassion and even a troubled spirit of His own. He acknowledges it when He arrives to see Mary and Martha and sees their pain. He is moved with compassion, and then He goes on to weep. He weeps for the sadness that the people feel and the darkness of death's power. Death is an enemy that has been causing this kind of pain in the lives of God's people for centuries, and the sadness it brings never ceases to grieve Jesus' heart. It grieves Him, in the same way, to see your daily sorrows even though He has a plan to redeem them all. He knows better than anyone what it is like to live between sorrow and redemption, and He does not pass over your pain.

But none of His tender compassion in the waiting in between can be divorced from His redemptive purposes for the end of all time. Throughout this passage in John, we hear glimmers of Jesus' redemption plan. He waited to heal Lazarus, not only to redeem that one man's life from physical death but to show forth His redemptive power and plan to all who were there and to all who would hear of this event. Even as He ministered to and wept with the grievers in their sorrow, He was working redemption and healing in the in-between for far more than the one who had died. He did not ignore the pain of the present to focus on the future of other people's souls. He used the brokenness of death, in His timing, to show forth His power for both the present and eternal needs of the people around Him. And He does the very same with our suffering. None of it is ever wasted.

Jesus came with redemption and comfort. He came bringing good news for Mary, Martha, and Lazarus, but He also brought His love and peace for the time in between. He waited to heal because His concern was for their eternal home and not just their temporal happiness. He used the darkness as a means to speak of His light as a hope for the present. This is how we too can fight back against the grief of brokenness. These same redemption promises for the in-between are the truths you can use to fight your depression. You need to engage actively and daily in this fight, wielding the truth of the gospel and the reality of your heavenly, redeemed future against the lies of the darkness that whisper promises of only present and future despair.

You need to fight in this way but not for the goal of ending your depression to prove your faith. Instead, you can exercise your faith by waging war on the enemy of your heart and mind who wants you to give in to despair. It is a present, daily fight during this in-between time. And it is in this fight that you reflect Jesus in your grieving while finding hope in the redemption to come. You may wage this battle your entire life, and that is okay because ending the fight on earth is not the goal. Rather, the goal is to fight faithfully until glory. And truly, it is the Lord who fights for you, and He has already won. His redemption plan is secure, and He is not late with the healing. The end is certain. His redemption of this darkness will be your eternal reality. In the meantime, you are being used here for His purposes with His comfort as an anchor through it all.

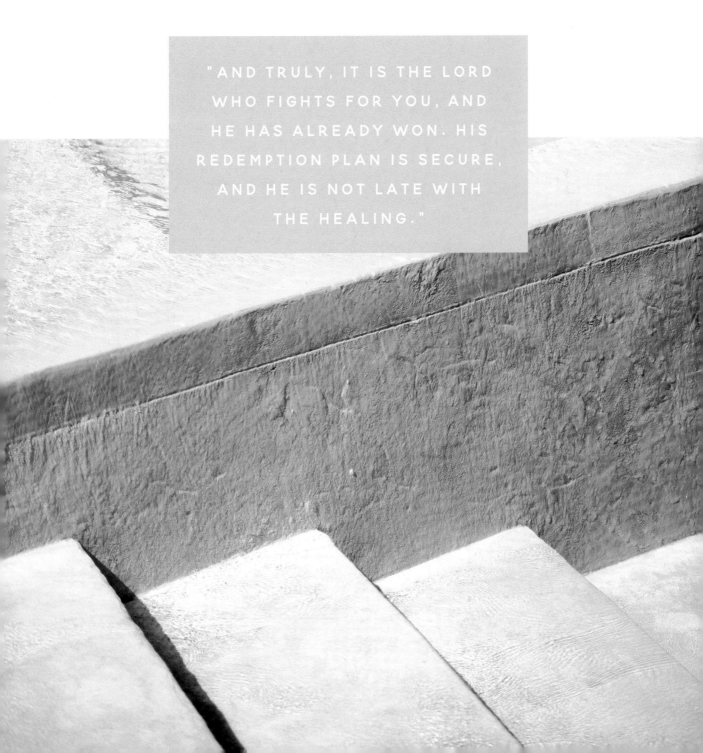

"AND TRULY, IT IS THE LORD WHO FIGHTS FOR YOU, AND HE HAS ALREADY WON. HIS REDEMPTION PLAN IS SECURE, AND HE IS NOT LATE WITH THE HEALING."

In what ways can you resonate with the response of Mary and Martha amid their pain? What pressing questions might you present to God in prayer about your own battle or someone else's battle with depression?

_____

_____

_____

_____

_____

_____

_____

_____

_____

How does Jesus respond to the hurt and grief caused by the death of Lazarus? What does this teach us about His character?

_____

_____

_____

_____

_____

_____

_____

_____

How can we remain active and hopeful in the fight against the sin and darkness of this world with Christ?

_____

_____

_____

_____

_____

_____

_____

"THE REALITY OF SIN IN THE WORLD
MEANS THAT EVERYTHING IS
FRACTURED — EVEN GOOD THINGS.
NOTHING IN THIS WORLD IS YET
AS IT SHOULD BE."

Jesus in the garden of gethsemane

Read: Matthew 26

Moments before His death, we get a close-up glimpse into the heart of Christ. He was in the garden of Gethsemane awaiting crucifixion and preparing to take on the sin of the entire world. The weight of humanity was on His shoulders, resulting in emotional turmoil. Jesus models purposeful intentionality amid His suffering. While we look outside of our depression for a hope to which we can cling, we are not encouraged to let our days pass aimlessly. We are called to our present circumstances, to make the most of our time, and to present ourselves as living sacrifices for Jesus Christ. This means that even our deepest sorrows can be used intentionally and purposefully to the glory of God. In the garden of Gethsemane, we are seamlessly presented with a model for walking through depression well as we look specifically at how Jesus walked through His grief and sorrow.

When chief priests and elders conspired to kill Jesus, Jesus was well aware of what was to come, even the timing of His death. You might imagine the thoughts and feelings that would surround knowing when your final hour would come. Perhaps you would have been overwhelmed, emotionally distraught, or wondering how to fill your final moments. How does Jesus initially respond? He continues teaching and walking with His disciples. He travels to Bethany alongside His disciples, and while there he interacts with a woman who anoints him with the finest perfume. Jesus uses this as an opportunity likely to point forward to His death and burial but also to commend her actions, even at the disciples' objections for bestowing Him with her finest gifts given out of reverence and honor. Shortly after, at the Passover, Jesus shares a meal with His disciples and notably introduces the first Lord's Supper. Here again, Jesus is using His last moments to teach and instruct His disciples.

Though His crucifixion loomed in the distance, Jesus was not deterred from pointing others to the hope of the gospel. He was faithful to continue the work He came to do. Depression may discourage us to the point of exhaustion or leave us feeling depleted with a lack of desire to attend church or engage in ministry efforts. But Jesus' response provides a powerful reminder that even amidst our darkest days, God's purpose for us on this earth remains the same. Should we let our feelings and circumstances dictate how we engage in the life of the church and the proclamation of the gospel, we might continually neglect and avoid these purposes. Even so, our prayers for strength and endurance in the middle of those feelings do not fall flat, and we can continually ask for help when tempted to abandon our ministry efforts.

After sharing His last meal with the disciples, Jesus went with them to the garden. In the moments before Jesus' pulling away to pray, He chose to spend His remaining time with His close friends. This is important to note. Jesus took with him Peter and the two sons of Zebedee (Matthew 26:37). He wanted to be with those whom He could trust and depend on to walk through the grief with Him. He did not take everyone with Him but only those He felt closest to. During their time together, he shared His sorrows and troubles and asked for their support and help, saying, "I am deeply grieved to the point of death. Remain here and stay awake with me" (Matthew 26:37-38). We are reminded through this chapter in Matthew that even Jesus found strength and comfort by walking with others through His suffering. Depression breeds the inclination to isolate ourselves. But even when our feelings aim to direct us otherwise, may we seek to surround ourselves with those who will bear our burdens with us, pray for us, comfort us with God's truth, and walk with us through the trenches. We need to invite those closest to us not only into the joys and victories but also into the uncomfortable and hard. As Charles H. Spurgeon explains, "Friendship is one of the sweetest joys of life. Many might have failed beneath the bitterness of their trial had they not found

a friend." May we exhaust the riches offered to us through friendship by honestly bearing our hearts to others and asking in humility for their support when we need it most.

Following time with His friends, Jesus pulled away and went to the Father in prayer. This is how He spent the majority of His time leading up to His death. In Luke 22, it is recorded that Jesus' mental anguish was so great that His sweat became like drops of blood. An innocent man bearing the sins of the world on His shoulders produced a severity of anguish that no other man has experienced. These final moments bring light to the tension we experience in this world. Of course, Jesus knew what He came to earth to do, and He knew the ultimate outcome and reward of His suffering. Yet, even Jesus did not walk to the cross with ease. He did not face His circumstances void of physical and emotional pain. He continually exposed His heart to the Father in prayer, crying out, "My Father, if it is possible, let this cup pass from me" (Matthew 26:39). At the height of our depression, we may pose similar questions to God. We may beg him to let these circumstances pass. We may plead for Him to bring us to the other side. This is a natural response in a fallen world. But what we see in the garden of Gethsemane is that there is a bigger story taking place, and God is using every single season and experience of our lives to shape it for His glory. God is taking the bitter and making it sweet. He is taking the turmoil and turning it into triumph. There is more to be seen than what we presently face. Just as Christ fought to fix His eyes on the glorious future grace that awaited Him on the other side of the cross—that which led Him to endure—now we can also fix our eyes on that same joy set before us.

Through his acquaintance with grief and sorrow, Jesus continued His ministry, found comfort among His closest friends, and continually spent time with the Father in prayer. Ultimately, Jesus chose to rest in the sovereign wisdom of God, looking beyond His own grief and bowing to the Father's will (Matthew 26:39). He claimed truth over His present circumstances, knowing that His suffering would pass and that He would soon be seated at the right hand of the Father. He believed what God promised to Him and walked willingly forward as He held onto that hope. We might be tempted to see these responses as an oversimplification of dealing with depression. But we are remiss to ignore the ways our sinless Savior sought strength and comfort in His suffering. Satan delights in minimizing the power and wisdom found in the many ways God offers us help and healing, and he will stop at nothing to lead us to doubt and turn away from the only One who can truly save and sustain us. God's Word continually reminds us of what is true and trustworthy, even when we are struggling to believe it. It reminds us of who God is and how He promises to care for us, even when Satan tempts us to think otherwise. The record of Jesus' final hours does not only offer us wisdom in how to walk through depression, but the result of Jesus' final hour secures us with His presence to help us along the way. His final words before He ascended to the right hand of the Father give us strength for today and bright and glorious hope for tomorrow: "And remember, I am with you always, to the end of the age" (Matthew 28:20).

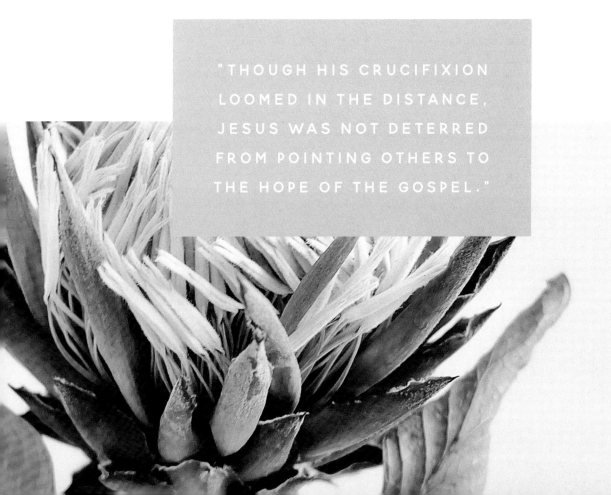

"THOUGH HIS CRUCIFIXION LOOMED IN THE DISTANCE, JESUS WAS NOT DETERRED FROM POINTING OTHERS TO THE HOPE OF THE GOSPEL."

In what specific ways does Jesus respond to His suffering?

_____

_____

_____

_____

_____

_____

_____

_____

_____

_____

How do these responses encourage you? What response do you find most difficult to emulate?

_____

_____

_____

_____

_____

_____

_____

_____

_____

_____

_____

What comfort do you find in the reality that even our sinless Savior experienced the same feelings that accompany depression?

_____

_____

_____

_____

_____

_____

_____

_____

_____

_____

_____

"THE RECORD OF JESUS' FINAL
HOURS DOES NOT ONLY OFFER
US WISDOM IN HOW TO WALK
THROUGH DEPRESSION, BUT THE
RESULT OF JESUS' FINAL HOUR
SECURES US WITH HIS PRESENCE
TO HELP US ALONG THE WAY."

THE ONLY QUALIFIER FOR
COMING TO CHRIST IS THAT WE
ARE WEARY AND BURDENED.

week 4 | *day 4*

who is Jesus in the midst of our depression?

Read: Matthew 11:28-30

When presented with biblical truths about Jesus amid our depression, we can sometimes depersonalize them. Even if we can acknowledge them intellectually to be true, we might wrestle with planting those truths deeply in our hearts and souls. This often leads to a disconnect in who Jesus is to us in the midst of our depression. We might readily understand Him as our Savior, accepting us through the gospel-saving work of salvation. We might even expectantly look to our future glory with Jesus when we will be like Him and dwell with Him. But we may struggle to connect with who Jesus is in the in-between. Who is Jesus in our sin and suffering? Who is He in our darkest hours when we do not want to get out of bed? Who is Jesus when the tears will not stop and the sadness overwhelms us? Who is Jesus when our Bibles are closed and our prayers are silent? We might be tempted to believe that Jesus is present only when we are at our best and most deserving of a relationship with Him. We might assume that we can only approach Him when we have cleaned ourselves up and are fully repentant. But the Bible speaks to the truth of who Jesus is to us in every moment.

We find a beautiful portrait of His heart in Matthew 11:28-30 which says, "Come to me, all of you who are weary and burdened, and I will give you rest. Take up my yoke and learn from me, because I am lowly and humble in heart, and you will find rest for your souls. For my yoke is easy and my burden is light." Jesus invites us to come to Him so that we might find rest for our souls, and how does He invite us to do so? He does not ask that we come to Him with strength and valor. He does not ask that we clean ourselves up. He does not ask that we attain righteousness of our own. The only qualifier for coming to Christ is that we are weary and burdened. He invites us as weak, unappealing, and having absolutely nothing to offer. And He delights in receiving us. This speaks volumes to the person of Jesus. The work of the gospel reminds us that while we were still ungodly, sinful, and enemies of God, Christ died for us. He died for us at our absolute worst. Such a sacrificial display is only enacted through a love more powerful and supernatural than anything we have ever known—a love that moved Christ from heaven to earth so that He could save us from our sins, a love that is humble, gentle, and selfless, a love that bears all, a love that continues to bring Christ near when our spirits are crushed and our souls are cast down, and a love that enables Christ to delight in continually doing so. Christ calls us to Him in love because He knows our deepest needs are met in Him, and He will stop at nothing to remind us of this truth.

When we come to Christ, He offers us rest. This is not a one-time transaction. It is not offered only when we respond to the gospel as a means of rest for weary souls in search of hope outside of this world, nor is it only offered as eternal rest when we enter into heaven's gates. It is a rest, present and readily available to us. It is a rest that combats the swirling thoughts of doubt and despair. It is a rest that surrounds us with solace when life feels all-consuming. When we find no strength or desire within ourselves, it is a rest that remains firmly planted in the sovereign promises of God. We must continually seek the Lord for rest and comfort in a discontented world. In our continual pursuit, Jesus is never exhausted by our need for rest in Him, and He never will be. When depression or another trial leads us to believe we have sought Jesus too much or asked Him to carry too much, we are gravely misunderstanding who He is. Who better and more willing to carry our sorrows than the One who took the sins of the world upon Himself? He has proven time and time again that He is more than capable of caring for us. Should we ever doubt His intent in such a sacrificial display toward us,

Jesus Himself reminds us of His heart for us in this passage. Being one who moves towards His people in love is the essence of who He is. He is compassionate and merciful toward the sin and sorrows of His people. This does not negate His judgment but reminds us that His natural inclination is to act humbly and mercifully. Judgment is the last lever because mercy is the first. Likely, our greatest obstruction to receiving the grace and mercy offered to us in Christ is our own misunderstanding of who He truly is.

So, who is Jesus in the midst of our depression? Scripture abounds with reminders of the Savior who has humbly and in love offered Himself to His people. He is everything He promised He would be. He is readily available to receive us (John 6:37), regardless of the baggage we bring with us. He is life-giving (John 10:10), giving purpose to our days even when they may seem empty and aimless. He is the author and perfecter of our faith (Hebrew 12:2), using every single opportunity to shape us into His likeness. He is our advocate (1 John 2:1), rising up to defend us in our failings based on the merits of His own suffering and death. He is our peace (Ephesians 2:14), bringing calm amid the waves and winds of our circumstances. He is our hope (1 Peter 1:3-4), piercing through even the darkest nights of depression to a bright and glorious new morning. Words are insufficient to explain who He is. We are best equipped to battle depression with Jesus Christ. Our tears are not ignored by Him. Our grief is not unknown by Him. Our sorrow is seen by Him. Our burdens are carried by Him. Our hope is secure in Him. May we run to Him without delay.

"WE ARE BEST EQUIPPED TO BATTLE DEPRESSION WITH JESUS CHRIST."

In what ways are you naturally inclined to think of Jesus in your sin and suffering? How does Matthew 11:28-30 affirm or refute those thoughts?

What does Jesus promise when we come to Him? In what ways might we create obstacles for ourselves in coming to Him?

Scripture abounds with reminders of who our Savior is. Adding to the passages presented in the study, take time to identify three passages of Scripture that tell us who Jesus Christ is to His people?

GOD CARES FOR OUR BODIES
BECAUSE HE CREATED THEM,
AND THEREFORE, HE WILL ONE
DAY SET THEM COMPLETELY FREE
FROM THE BONDAGE OF SIN.

week 4 | day 5

what Jesus' second coming means for our depression

Read: 1 Corinthians 15

Throughout this study, we have referenced the future glory in Christ as a healing hope amid our battle with depression. This truth cannot sit on our hearts enough. We are deemed utterly hopeless without it. It is everything we strive for as Christians and serves as an anchor for our souls in this life and the next. As we recognize and name our personal experiences with depression, as well as the experiences of others, we will learn that everyone has a different story. For some, by God's grace, we may see the end of our depression in this lifetime. It may be short-lived or circumstantial, leaving us the opportunity to comfort others who continue to endure it. For others, we may ebb and flow through seasons of depression and its tendencies, never fully experiencing its end this side of heaven. It may be clinical or causeless, like an ever-looming cloud that leaves us searching for a brighter day. Though we may all have a different story about how depression takes form in our lives, in Christ, we find our way to the same ending. God promises the ultimate fulfillment of the hope He has offered us in Jesus Christ. He will come again and fully and finally bring restoration and redemption. Jesus' resurrection defeated death once and for all. Therefore, Christians no longer fear death, for just as they die to themselves, they are raised with Christ to walk in the newness of life. And when Christ returns, all of His people will be raised with Him. The second coming of Jesus Christ will be a personal and visible display of all that He has promised His people through salvation. Every knee will bow, and every tongue will confess that He is Lord! He will receive all the praise and honor and glory due His name, and He will consummate the kingdom rule of God in its fullness (Hebrew 9:28).

The glorious reality of the second coming of Christ is that we will experience the full redemption and glorification of our bodies. We see evidence of this in Philippians 3:20-21 which tells us, "our citizenship is in heaven, and we eagerly wait for a Savior from there, the Lord Jesus Christ. He will transform the body of our humble condition into the likeness of his glorious body, by the power that enables him to subject everything to himself." Our broken and imbalanced bodies will be transformed and made new. Can you imagine? The sin we wrestle with, the addictions that creep in, the lies that tempt us to despair, the impulses we struggle to control—these and all other physical or emotional failings will be no more. We will know God fully, experience every emotion in the way God intended, reside in a bodily home perfected by glory, and live in sinless delight! God cares for our bodies because He created them, and therefore, He will one day set them completely free from the bondage of sin. His ultimate goal for our physical, emotional, and spiritual being is that we would reflect the image of His perfect Son. This can encourage and empower us as we wrestle with the reality of our current limitations amid depression, looking toward the hope of the redemption of our bodies. As believers wait for the culmination of this promise, we are not left in limbo but are equipped and strengthened by the indwelling of the Holy Spirit who serves as a seal—a guarantee of our inheritance until we acquire possession of this glorious hope (Ephesians 1:13-14).

The promise of Christ's return changes everything about the way we can continue to persevere through depression. Contrary to what our thoughts and feelings may lead us to believe, we are not crushed or defeated by the reality of depression in our lives. It may provide more obstacles, weigh heavily on our lives, or make our days feel significantly more difficult to handle. But, the hope of Christ is that we are never forgotten or forsaken. Even in our affliction, we are being renewed day by day in preparation for an eternal weight of glory that cannot compare to the battles we face today (2 Corinthians 4:16-18). And we are sustained by the joy that was purchased for us through salvation—a joy that holds a flame to the shadows and reminds us to keep pressing onward. Because when we arrive at eternity's shore there will be no more tears, no more sorrows, no more darkness, but only bursting light and lasting joy that will never be taken from us (John 16:22). Death will be defeated, and we will know life eternal. We will sing, rejoice, dance, and praise the Lord with our entire being, nothing hindering us from fully enjoying the presence of God forever.

This is the hope Christ brings to all who encounter and suffer depression. Hope in Christ leads us to trust that the true and worthy judge will deal justly with this world according to His truth. Hope in Christ points us to the sovereignty of God when questions are left unanswered. Hope in Christ secures our peace and joy when we are tempted to despair. Hope in Christ ignites our endurance in a way that gives us purpose to face another day in pursuit of holiness and preparation for the day of the Lord. Hope in Christ fuels our faith to face every dark night, scheme of Satan, or affliction of this world. Hope in Christ turns our mourning into jubilation, our suffering into purpose, and our shame into glory. May we ever abide in the promises of Christ's return and the hope that follows. Christian, depression will not have the final say in your life, Christ will.

"DEPRESSION WILL NOT HAVE THE FINAL SAY IN YOUR LIFE, CHRIST WILL."

What is your understanding of the second coming of Christ? How does it speak to the pangs of depression?

What will happen to our bodies when Christ returns? In what specific ways does the hope of glorified bodies speak into your present circumstances?

Continued on next page

How does Christ's victory over death and sin equip you, even in depression, to answer the charge at the end of 1 Corinthians 15 to be "steadfast, immovable, always excelling in the Lord's work, because you know that your labor in the Lord is not in vain"?

_____

_____

_____

_____

_____

_____

Write a prayer asking that the truths uncovered through this study would meet you in a deep and personal way and would help you compassionately minister to others.

_____

_____

_____

_____

_____

_____

_____

_____

_____

_____

_____

_____

SUMMARIZING THOUGHTS:

week four
memory
verse

-

FOR WE KNOW THAT THE WHOLE

CREATION HAS BEEN GROANING

TOGETHER WITH LABOR PAINS

UNTIL NOW. NOT ONLY THAT,

BUT WE OURSELVES WHO HAVE THE

SPIRIT AS THE FIRSTFRUITS — WE ALSO

GROAN WITHIN OURSELVES,

EAGERLY WAITING FOR ADOPTION,

THE REDEMPTION OF OUR BODIES.

-

ROMANS 8:22-23

week four
reflection

Write a brief summary of this week's passages.

_____

_____

_____

_____

_____

_____

_____

_____

_____

What did you observe about God and His character from these passages?

_____

_____

_____

_____

_____

What do these passages teach you about the condition of mankind and about yourself?

_____

_____

_____

_____

_____

How do these passages point to the gospel?

_____

_____

_____

_____

_____

How should you respond to these passages? What is the personal application?

_____

_____

_____

_____

_____

_____

What specific action steps can you take this week to apply these passages?

_____

_____

_____

_____

_____

ADDITIONAL
RESOURCES

Charles Spurgeon

CHARLES HADDON SPURGEON WAS BORN IN KELVEDON, A VILLAGE IN ENGLAND, ON JUNE 19, 1834. NAMED THE PRINCE OF PREACHERS, HE WAS ONE OF THE MOST INFLUENTIAL CHRISTIAN PREACHERS OF HIS TIME, AND HIS INFLUENCE CONTINUES EVEN TO THIS DAY.

Spurgeon came to know the Lord around the age of fifteen. When caught in a snowstorm and stepping into a chapel for shelter, a preacher spoke on Isaiah 45:22 which says, "Turn to me and be saved, all the ends of the earth. For I am God, and there is no other." The preacher spoke directly to Spurgeon, inviting him to look to Christ and live. From that moment, Spurgeon's life was changed, and the remainder of his years would be simply characterized by his unbending devotion to look to Christ for all of life. Shortly after salvation, he began preaching and teaching regularly. Without any formal education, he led a remarkable preaching career. By the age of twenty, he had preached over 600 times, and by the end of his life, he had written 139 books with 63 volumes of published sermons. Spurgeon happily married Susannah Thompson in 1856, and the two welcomed twin sons the following year.

Throughout all of his successes and joys, many are surprised to know that Spurgeon knew well the pain and despair of depression. There were several events and occurrences that took place in his life to enhance the pains and trials he experienced. On one account in 1856, Spurgeon preached to a large crowd of over 20,000. While praying, the structural support of the building began to give way due to a fire, killing seven people and injuring 28 others. Spurgeon later recounts the incident: "I was pressed beyond measure and out of bounds with an enormous weight of misery. The tumult, the panic, the deaths, were day and night before me, and made life a burden" (*Lectures to My Students* by C.H. Spurgeon). The trauma that followed such an event provided great mental suffering for Spurgeon as he continued to teach and preach.

Additionally, Spurgeon dealt with the physical ailments of his wife, Susannah. Spurgeon's wife suffered from severe medical issues and spent much of her adult life weak and disabled. Her issues became so severe that she needed to have surgery, and the results were devastating after a botched operation. As Spurgeon sought to care for her, he faced his own physical issues, suffering from gout at the age of 35. He remarked on the yearly effects of such a disease, saying:

"I had nothing I could say to God but this, 'Thou art my Father, and I am thy child and thou, as a Father art tender and full of mercy.' I could not bear to see my child suffer as thou makest me suffer, and if I saw him tormented as I am now, I would do what I could to help him, and put my arms under him to sustain him. Wilt thou hide thy face from me, my Father? Wilt thou still lay on a heavy hand, and not give me a smile from thy countenance?" (*Anguish and Agonies of Charles Spurgeon* by Darrel Amundson)

He wrestled with his realities. His pain continued, and the necessary time it took to recover and rest grew more frequent.

Plenty of Spurgeon's circumstances were attributed to his battle with depression, but his struggle also entailed seasons when there was no clear source. At an early age, Spurgeon shared, "My spirits were sunken so low that I could weep by the hour like a child, and not know what I wept for" (*Charles Spurgeon* by John Piper). He shared that these bouts of depression could not be reasoned with. They were causeless and undefinable and required a supernatural, heavenly hand to do away with them. Thus Spurgeon's greatest help amid depression was his ultimate hope in Christ. Through all of the tragedies, physical ailments, pressures of life and ministry, and unexplained feelings of despair, he found purpose in his sufferings. He believed that God was sovereign over his sorrows, noting that though affliction was bitter to the taste, tracing it to its source at the throne of God would provide sweet and life-giving water. He was sustained by what he believed to be true of God, even when his feelings and circumstances tempted him to believe otherwise.

Spurgeon's life and battle with depression curated a deep dependence on the Lord for strength and endurance. We have much wisdom to glean from his faithfulness amid despair. He held fast to the gospel of Jesus Christ to provide hope and help throughout his suffering. This is evident not only in the recounting of his life but also in the records of his preaching, teaching, and writing.

His suffering allowed him to be deeply humbled in service and reverence of the Lord. In turn, he used his suffering as a means to minister to and bless others through various means. He was able to minister with compassion and comfort to those who faced similar trials and circumstances, claiming that he would go into the deep a hundred times if it meant he was able to comfort and cheer on one downcast soul.

A testament to Spurgeon's faith through his suffering is profoundly represented in his final sermon preached on June 7, 1891, before his final breath in January of 1892. He said:

> He is the most magnanimous of captains. There never was his like among the choicest of princes. He is always to be found in the thickest part of the battle. When the wind blows cold he always takes the bleak side of the hill. The heaviest end of the cross lies ever on his shoulders. If he bids us carry a burden, he carries it also. If there is anything that is gracious, generous, kind, and tender, yea lavish and superabundant in love, you always find it in him. These forty years and more have I served him, blessed be his name! and I have had nothing but love from him. I would be glad to continue yet another forty years in the same dear service here below if so it pleased him. His service is life, peace, joy. Oh, that you would enter it at once! God help you to enlist under the banner of Jesus even this day! Amen. ("The Statute of David for the Sharing of the Spoil")

There is a Fountain

BY WILLIAM COWPER

There is a fountain filled with blood,
Drawn from Immanuel's veins,
And sinners plunged beneath that flood
Lose all their guilty stains:
Lose all their guilty stains,
Lose all their guilty stains;
And sinners plunged beneath that flood
Lose all their guilty stains.

The dying thief rejoiced to see
That fountain in His day;
And there have I, though vile as he,
Washed all my sins away:
Washed all my sins away,
Washed all my sins away;
And there have I, though vile as he,
Washed all my sins away.

Dear dying Lamb, Thy precious blood
Shall never lose its pow'r,
Till all the ransomed church of God
Are safe, to sin no more:
Are safe, to sin no more,
Are safe, to sin no more;
Till all the ransomed church of God
Are safe, to sin no more.

E'er since by faith I saw the stream
Thy flowing wounds supply,
Redeeming love has been my theme,
And shall be till I die:
And shall be till I die,
And shall be till I die;
Redeeming love has been my theme,
And shall be till I die.

When this poor, lisping, stamm'ring tongue
Lies silent in the grave,
Then in a nobler, sweeter song,
I'll sing Thy pow'r to save:
I'll sing Thy pow'r to save,
I'll sing Thy pow'r to save;
Then in a nobler, sweeter song,
I'll sing Thy pow'r to save.

Read or listen to the previous hymn. Use this page to respond to the lyrics. Journal through each line, write out a prayerful response, or accompany the lyrics with words of Scripture.

God Moves in a Mysterious Way

BY WILLIAM COWPER

God moves in a mysterious way
His wonders to perform;
He plants His footsteps in the sea
And rides upon the storm.

Deep in unfathomable mines
Of never failing skill
He treasures up His bright designs
And works His sovereign will.

Ye fearful saints, fresh courage take;
The clouds ye so much dread
Are big with mercy and shall break
In blessings on your head.

Judge not the Lord by feeble sense,
But trust Him for His grace;
Behind a frowning providence
He hides a smiling face.

His purposes will ripen fast,
Unfolding every hour;
The bud may have a bitter taste,
But sweet will be the flow'r.

Blind unbelief is sure to err
And scan His work in vain;
God is His own interpreter,
And He will make it plain.

Read or listen to the previous hymn. Use this page to respond to the lyrics. Journal through each line, write out a prayerful response, or accompany the lyrics with words of Scripture.

It is Well

BY HORATIO SPAFFORD

When peace, like a river, attendeth
my way,
When sorrows like sea billows roll;
Whatever my lot, Thou hast taught
me to say,
It is well, it is well with my soul.

Refrain:
It is well with my soul,
It is well, it is well with my soul.

Though Satan should buffet,
though trials should come,
Let this blest assurance control,
That Christ hath regarded my
helpless estate,
And hath shed His own blood
for my soul.
My sin—oh, the bliss of this
glorious thought!—
My sin, not in part but the whole,
Is nailed to the cross, and I bear
it no more,
Praise the Lord, praise the Lord,
O my soul!

For me, be it Christ, be it Christ
hence to live:
If Jordan above me shall roll,
No pang shall be mine, for in
death as in life
Thou wilt whisper Thy peace
to my soul.

But, Lord, 'tis for Thee, for Thy
coming we wait,
The sky, not the grave, is our goal;
Oh, trump of the angel! Oh, voice
of the Lord!
Blessed hope, blessed rest of my soul!

And Lord, haste the day when the
faith shall be sight,
The clouds be rolled back as a scroll;
The trump shall resound, and the
Lord shall descend,
Even so, it is well with my soul.

Read or listen to the previous hymn. Use this page to respond to the lyrics. Journal through each line, write out a prayerful response, or accompany the lyrics with words of Scripture.

what is
the gospel?

THANK YOU FOR READING AND ENJOYING THIS STUDY WITH US! WE ARE
ABUNDANTLY GRATEFUL FOR THE WORD OF GOD, THE INSTRUCTION WE
GLEAN FROM IT, AND THE EVER-GROWING UNDERSTANDING ABOUT
GOD'S CHARACTER FROM IT. WE ARE ALSO THANKFUL THAT SCRIPTURE
CONTINUALLY POINTS TO ONE THING IN INNUMERABLE WAYS: THE GOSPEL.

We remember our brokenness when we read about the fall of Adam and Eve in the garden of Eden (Genesis 3), when sin entered into a perfect world and maimed it. We remember the necessity that something innocent must die to pay for our sin when we read about the atoning sacrifices in the Old Testament. We read that we have all sinned and fallen short of the glory of God (Romans 3:23) and that the penalty for our brokenness, the wages of our sin, is death (Romans 6:23). We all are in need of grace and mercy, but most importantly, we all need a Savior.

We consider the goodness of God when we realize that He did not plan to leave us in this dire state. We see His promise to buy us back from the clutches of sin and death in Genesis 3:15. And we see that promise accomplished with Jesus Christ on the cross. Jesus Christ knew no sin yet became sin so that we might become righteous through His sacrifice (2 Corinthians 5:21). Jesus was tempted in every way that we are and lived sinlessly. He was reviled yet still yielded Himself for our sake, that we may have life abundant in Him. Jesus lived the perfect life that we could not live and died the death that we deserved.

The gospel is profound yet simple. There are many mysteries in it that we can never exhaust this side of heaven, but there is still overwhelming weight to its implications in this life. The gospel is the telling of our sinfulness and God's goodness, and this gracious gift compels a response. We are saved by grace through faith, which means that we rest with faith in the grace that Jesus Christ displayed on the cross (Ephesians 2:8-9). We cannot save ourselves from our brokenness or do any amount of good works to merit God's favor, but we can have faith that what Jesus accomplished in His death, burial, and resurrection was more than enough for our salvation and our eternal delight. When we accept God, we are commanded to die to our self and our sinful desires and live a life worthy of the calling we have received (Ephesians 4:1). The gospel compels us to be sanctified, and in so doing, we are conformed to the likeness of Christ Himself. This is hope. This is redemption. This is the gospel.

SCRIPTURE TO REFERENCE:

GENESIS 3:15 — *I will put hostility between you and the woman, and between your offspring and her offspring. He will strike your head, and you will strike his heel.*

ROMANS 3:23 — *For all have sinned and fall short of the glory of God;*

ROMANS 6:23 — *For the wages of sin is death, but the gift of God is eternal life in Christ Jesus our Lord.*

2 CORINTHIANS 5:21 — *He made the one who did not know sin to be sin for us, so that in him we might become the righteousness of God.*

EPHESIANS 2:8-9 — *For you are saved by grace through faith, and this is not from yourselves; it is God's gift—not from works, so that no one can boast.*

EPHESIANS 4:1 — *Therefore I, the prisoner in the Lord, urge you to walk worthy of the calling you have received,*

*Thank you for studying
God's Word with us!*

CONNECT WITH US

@thedailygraceco

@kristinschmucker

CONTACT US

info@thedailygraceco.com

SHARE

#thedailygraceco

#lampandlight

VISIT US ONLINE

thedailygraceco.com

MORE DAILY GRACE

The Daily Grace App
Daily Grace Podcast